MARRIAGE RESCUE

MARRIAGE RESCUE

*Overcoming Ten Deadly Sins
in Failing Relationships*

Gary Direnfeld, MSW, RSW

NEW HORIZON PRESS
Far Hills, New Jersey

Requests for permission should be addressed to:

New Horizon Press
P.O. Box 669
Far Hills, NJ 07931

Direnfeld, Gary
Marriage Rescue: Overcoming Ten Deadly Sins in Failing Relationships

Cover design: Wendy Bass
Interior design: Scribe Inc.

Library of Congress Control Number: 2012945205

ISBN-13: 978-0-88282-430-7
New Horizon Press

Manufactured in the U.S.A.

17   16   15   14   13   1   2   3   4   5

Author's Note

This book is based on the author's research, personal experience, interviews and real-life experiences. The couples' stories presented represent a compilation of issues taken from the author's thirty years as a social worker. No one story represents a single case. In order to protect privacy, names have been changed and identifying characteristics have been altered except for contributing experts. The facts represented and names used do not reveal any single couple or person directly.

For purposes of simplifying usage, the pronouns his/her and s/he are sometimes used interchangeably. The information contained herein is not meant to be a substitute for professional evaluation and therapy with mental health professionals.

Contents

Introduction

Imagine having the kind of marriage where you wake up each morning feeling thrilled with the person lying beside you. Imagine feeling completely supported by your partner. Imagine having plenty of things to talk about and that at the end of each workday, when you find yourselves both at home, you are happy to embrace and chat about the day's events. Imagine looking forward to vacations together. Imagine the scene in old age, sitting in rockers side by side, hand in hand.

However, if you have chosen to read *Marriage Rescue*, it's likely the reality is very different.

It's probable that for a number of reasons your marriage may be on a downslide and you are feeling desperate. Even if your marriage is not deteriorating, it's likely you are not finding the kind of marital satisfaction that you dreamed would follow your wedding or moving in together.

It may be that your marriage was never on track: your issues predate your wedding and you deluded yourself into believing that getting married would reset the problems of the past and make all things right. If not married, the same applies: It may be that your relationship was never on track and you believed that moving in together would right the wrongs and make everything better.

It may be that unforeseeable events have broadsided your marriage and sent it for a tumble. It may be that you and your spouse didn't get to know each other long enough before tying the knot and now, only after your wedding, what you have learned about each other is undesirable. It may be that you feel you and your partner have outgrown each other and no longer have anything in common. Perhaps there were a number of conversations never had, where you and your spouse find yourselves on opposite sides of the fence for issues never broached.

Whatever your marital issues, all you can do so far is imagine the kind of marriage or relationship you wish you had.

I am a social worker by profession and I have been assisting couples with getting along and feeling better about themselves for over thirty years. I have helped couples have the kinds of marriages and relationships of which they only dreamed.

There are a great many things that continue to bring men and women into therapy time after time. I have come to distinguish patterns and recognize that the vast majority of couples' relationship problems can be distilled into common major issues: the ten deadly sins of failing relationships.

I am going to share my knowledge about the ten deadly sins with you and provide you the same kind of insights and advice I provide my clients. In this book I believe you will learn something about yourself, your situation and your relationship. Through looking at the many examples of other couples with relationship problems, you will have an opportunity to examine yourself and your partner and figure out how you might do things differently to improve your relationship.

We will search the marital journeys of different couples and view their roles in relationships. I feel strongly that you will see yourself in one of these stories and, I hope, identify with at least one of the individuals to some degree. Indeed, you may see different parts of yourself or your situation in several of the stories.

If you find yourself wishing for a mutually-satisfying marriage where each partner completes the other, but you are not finding satisfaction or fulfillment in your current relationship, then this book is for you. However, before you have any illusions that all it takes is three clicks of your heels to have that fantasy life, think again. Great marriages take effort.

If you really want your marriage to work, if you want to get it back on track, then you and your partner are going to have to work hard to put your relationship there. Even if it's never a great marriage, you can certainly achieve a better marriage than you have right now. But there has to be a genuine commitment from both sides to make it happen.

There is an important prerequisite to beginning that work. Even though it takes both spouses to make it happen, each of you needs to realize that the first step is to get your ego out of the way. You likely have convinced yourself that everything would be better if only your spouse would change. But the truth is that until you take responsibility for your own contribution to distress, your marriage or relationship will never improve. Be prepared, because as you continue to read this book, much of the work will be focused on both of you managing yourselves differently in lieu of seeking to fix your partner.

You will learn to unravel the problems associated with each deadly sin of marital turmoil. You will learn to determine your contribution to the problem and from where your contribution stems. Then you will discover how to craft your own solutions given the uniqueness of your particular situation. Even if the issue you are grappling with in your marriage is not specifically one of the ten deadly sins, by reading this book you will still learn the skills and develop the strategies needed to address any issues interfering with your marriage. Each partner can achieve some degree of insight into him or herself.

Remember, though, a theme throughout this book is your taking responsibility for your contribution to marital or relationship distress. As much as you may gain insight into the behavior of your partner, nothing changes unless you first take responsibility for your contribution. This book is not about how you can go about changing your partner without examining yourself first. If you are sincere about improving your marriage and you're prepared to take responsibility for your own issues and work hard, then review the deadly sins, preferably with your partner.

Compare what you learn about yourselves and be prepared to discuss and then make significant changes to how you both go about doing things. Action will mean everything. This book is not just about contemplation and realizing the reasons for your marital strife, but also about developing new sets of behaviors that will save your relationship from its downslide and give you a shot at the kind of marriage of which you've only dreamed.

From the many couples experiencing marital discord I've counseled, I've learned that the severity of the problem is not the best indicator of whether or not a marriage can be rescued. I've seen marriages and relationships torn apart by seemingly minor issues. I've seen marriages fractured by issues from multiple affairs to drug and alcohol abuse to domestic violence that, as a result of hard work by the partners, were not only rescued but also rejoiced in as the relationships changed for the better.

Be aware that you can never tell at first glance whose marriage is going to make it and whose marriage is going to fail. In my years as a social worker, I have seen that there is only one factor that seems to determine success and failure: the willingness of both spouses to take responsibility, change and/or learn new behavior and leave their egos behind.

My style of marriage/relationship counseling is brief. Fifty percent of the people I see in counseling I only see once; not because it wasn't helpful, but because it *was* helpful. Couples counseling with me is not an exercise in navel gazing. There is no droning on about who is more to blame and there is no going around in circles wondering who has to change first.

Couples counseling with me as the therapist is a very intense experience for the couple. My first and, as I said, often only session with a client is on average three hours long, not the standard fifty-minute session where the client comes back week after week and where the first part of the next session is lost to the reminder of what was discussed previously. My clients do not sit arguing back and forth, discussing the "same old, same old" as they might between themselves. I take the couples through a very structured "get to know you" process where I ask a multitude of probing questions. Afterward I provide my insights as to the issues troubling the relationship and then offer my very direct guidance as to what the spouses should do differently to improve matters.

It always remains the couple's choice whether or not to believe my explanations for their distress or follow through with my suggestions. But those who do accept my explanations and do make use of my guidance typically improve their relationships much more successfully than those who do not. Some couples return for more sessions, but likely not the next week or the week after. I give them time, often several weeks, before they return. This way my feedback and guidance have the opportunity to percolate and they can follow through on directives aimed at improving matters.

If a couple does return and I discover they haven't followed through on the work, their time with me is limited. It is not much good meeting to review progress if the couple hasn't worked on anything from which to derive progress. Indeed, I am more apt to fire a client than a client is to fire me, and the thing that will have me terminate service is the client not doing the work. I am not here just to register clients' complaints, but hopefully to help them resolve their complaints. If they are not meeting me halfway by doing their part, I don't see much reason in continuing. When they come to me, I have a high expectation that clients will engage in the work of improving their relationship. As much as I can provide by way of insight, feedback and guidance, the real magic is in what the clients take away and in what the clients do differently thereafter. Don't do differently, don't expect change. Do differently, expect change.

This approach to counseling informs this book. You will have to look in the mirror and ask yourself, *What do I have to do differently in view of an unsatisfying relationship?* If you are prepared to ask yourself that, then you are prepared to begin this book in earnest.

In the next chapters we focus on the ten most common categories of problem areas I see in my counseling practice with couples. Each deadly sin alone is enough to ruin a relationship. For each sin, I reveal the sinner's motto. The motto is the one line that best encapsulates the attitude of the sinner. At the end of each chapter I provide a new motto to help you go from relationship sinner to relationship winner.

If you have previously been or are currently involved in any kind of inappropriate activity, you must be prepared to put an end to it immediately. If you're in an extramarital relationship, it will have to end. If you are using drugs and/or alcohol, be prepared to deal with it and enter sobriety. You need to start this process with both eyes open, realistically and with no other encumbrances. This is not about flirting with change, this is about making change.

As you continue with this book, be ready for self-examination, hard work and real change, not the illusion of change. Get ready to tackle the ten deadly sins which plague marital relationships.

Blaming

The Sinner's Motto:
It's not me; it's you.

When couples are in conflict, they often feel they are experts on their partners' contributions to the distress. Married couples in distress are keen to point their fingers at each other but almost never at themselves.

COUNSELING AND COUPLE DISTRESS

When I meet couples for the first time I tell them that I absolutely will listen to their complaints about each other. However, while doing so, I'm really interested in figuring out each person's contribution to distress. If partners don't take responsibility for their contributions to distress, no matter how big or small, things won't improve.

Imagine that a person goes to the doctor for treatment for a nasty sore throat. In pain, the person asks the doctor for a heavy-duty lozenge. Before the doctor can prescribe some medication, he first examines the patient. The doctor asks all the right questions about medical history, takes the patient's pulse and listens to the patient's heart. Finally, the doctor concurs. That's a nasty sore throat and the doctor is prepared to offer a prescription. However, the doctor looks the patient in the eyes and says, "I'll give you a prescription, but you must quit smoking."

Depending on the patient, the doctor will probably get one of three replies: In one scenario the patient says, "My goodness, I didn't realize that my smoking did this to me." This patient, taken aback by the doctor's words, may seek to quit smoking immediately, now understanding that his or her own bad habit caught up with him or her. This is the patient who will ask for help to quit smoking, who, by the time he or she leaves the office, is already doing better, just by heeding the doctor's initial advice and being so willing to change a harmful behavior.

In another scenario the patient may attempt to argue with the physician that he or she has been smoking for twenty years. The doctor will explain to the patient that smoking has finally caught up with the patient. The doctor may add, "If you continue to smoke, you run the risk of that sore throat turning into cancer." This patient may want to minimize the doctor's feedback, so rather than quitting smoking immediately, he or she tinkers with the advice. This patient may try to reduce his or her smoking habit, but otherwise still continues to smoke, just not as much. This patient is the consummate negotiator, toying with how much bad behavior he or she can get away with. This is the patient who thinks that through negotiation he or she can have it both ways. The patient provides the illusion of change, but instead of truly improving his or her health only delays the inevitable, succumbing to an ailment that, if taken seriously and tackled directly, would be likely to heal.

The last scenario has the patient look the doctor in the eyes and proclaim the doctor a quack. This patient disputes the diagnosis and explains that he or she has been a heavy smoker for twenty years and that it's never bothered him or her before and further, the only reason that he or she has a sore throat is because of the change of weather. This is a person who does not want to accept the feedback, does not want to change and does not want to accept any responsibility for his or her own contribution to his or her distress. The doctor may try to explain to the patient how he or she is wrong, that this is good medical information and that if the person continues to smoke, more harm will likely come. However, accepting or rejecting the information, smoking or quitting, is up to the patient and this patient doesn't listen well to anyone, particularly someone with a point of view that challenges his or her own. There is no room in the person's psyche for the input of others. The likelihood of this patient improving is very remote.

This is how some men and women enter into counseling. They seek help for their problems and to varying degrees they are willing to take responsibility for their contributions to distress. They easily advise of the issues originating with their partners but are less adept at discussing their own issues and taking responsibility.

YOUR PARTNER AND YOU

Many spouses argue that if their behavior does contribute to distress, then their contributions are minimal compared to that of their partners. The rationale here is, *As bad as I may be, my partner is worse.*

The truth of the matter, though, is that if things are to change, both individuals must take responsibility for their respective contributions to distress. It may not be an equal contribution, but admit your faults and be prepared to take some responsibility.

If you think a small contribution is inconsequential, consider this story: In my spare time I like to boat. I keep my boat at a small marina. A few slips down from where my boat is docked, another boater was doing his own repairs. His was an old boat and the floorboards were rotted. He meticulously removed the rotting floorboards and replaced them with new wood. It looked like he did a beautiful job. A week later though, when I came to look in on my boat, I saw his half submerged. I learned afterwards that when he repaired his boat, he breached the hull with a screw. Unbelievably, the breach was miniscule, about the size of the tip of a pen. What I learned from this is that a breach as seemingly insignificant as the tip of a pen, over time, is enough to sink a twenty-one-foot boat.

Personal behavior works the same way. Even when seemingly insignificant, an inappropriate behavior can sink a relationship over time. It really doesn't matter how big or small a person considers his or her own contribution to distress to be. What matters is that spouses take responsibility for their contributions, no matter the size.

DISRESPECTFUL BEHAVIOR AND MARITAL DISTRESS

Marital distress is fraught with disrespectful behavior. Taking responsibility for your contribution to distress is respectful of your partner. A good place to start when seeking to improve a marriage or relationship is with the respectful behavior of being accountable for your contribution. It really doesn't matter if you assess your contribution to be 1 percent, 50 percent or 90 percent. Whatever percentage your contribution is, given enough time, it can ruin your marriage. Be respectful and take responsibility for it.

In a situation such as an abusive marriage, where the abuse is one-sided and the other partner is the victim, the contribution by the victim may simply be his or her availability. If you are the victim, you still need to look at your contribution and consider, *Given the behavior of my partner, why do I continue to pursue the relationship? What is it about me that I can't let go? Why do I stay? What can I do differently, if not for my relationship then for myself? How can I be safe?*

LACK OF AWARENESS

The problem for some people is that they don't recognize their contribution to distress and the reason for this isn't necessarily complicated. Sometimes it's as simple as realizing that people grow so accustomed to their problems that they don't perceive them.

One day my sister-in-law told me that I had bad breath. Meeting with so many people as I do in my profession, the last thing I want is offensive breath. Now I carry a breath freshener. I changed my behavior, the result of some less-than-flattering feedback that was well-intentioned and in my personal interest. I was pleased my sister-in-law was comfortable enough to risk telling me what she did. I thanked her for this information. If you are told that something is offensive, accept it instructionally and do something about it.

Another example occurred on a trip my family took to California. Each winter, my family visited my parents in Palm Springs. We made plans to take a flight into Los Angeles, rent a car and drive the rest of the way to spend a week in the desert sun. As the airplane came over the mountains with Los Angeles in sight, I could see a brown haze surrounding the city; the pollution was obvious. The plane landed and by the time we retrieved our baggage and arrived at the rental car counter, my allergies were bothering me. My eyes were itchy and my throat scratchy. Looking at the clerk for both solace and to commiserate, I asked, "How can you stand the pollution?"

Bewildered, the clerk looked at me and asked, "What pollution?"

This person, who grew up in Los Angeles and was accustomed to the air quality, couldn't make sense of my distress. Not appreciating the impact of the pollution upon me, the clerk really thought I had a problem when the first words out of my mouth were a complaint.

Although accustomed to the pollution, the clerk was still affected by it. His risk of respiratory disease was greater than that of people living elsewhere, for no other reason than living in an area with heavy pollution. This was true with or without the clerk's realizing it. Lack of awareness of a problem doesn't mean the problem doesn't exist. Not being aware of one's contribution to distress doesn't mean that one isn't contributing to it. It just means one isn't aware of it.

If you want to have an appreciation of your contribution to distress or if you don't understand it so far, then you might have to do some soul searching to figure out yourself. What you are looking for is personal or interpersonal pollution. You need to examine yourself and ask, *What is it about myself that could bring distress to someone else, in particular, my partner?*

Here is a clue as to how to answer that question: Start by looking at your family history.

LOOK AT YOUR FAMILY

I refer to families as *ponds*. Did you grow up in a polluted pond? To determine if your pond was polluted, consider these questions: How did your parents get along? Did they fight? If so, what did it look like? Was there yelling or screaming, pushing or shoving? Did your parents call each other names? Were there any periods of time when they didn't speak to each other? If so, how did they come to start talking again? Did they ignore the rift or talk about it?

More than anything else, how your parents or care providers managed and resolved conflict will provide the biggest clue as to how you deal with conflict too. Do you try to resolve conflict or run from it? Further, the issues your parents fought about, you are also at risk of fighting about. A good clue to your issues will come in the form of examining your parents and their issues. Other aspects include alcohol, drugs, affairs, parenting styles and money. How did your parents handle these concerns?

There are some people who argue that they are nothing like their parents and that they have made conscious choices about that, understanding the issues of their parents.

For instance, in counseling I have worked with men who have reflected upon their fathers' abusive behaviors and have vowed to be different. However, some of these men are different only in intensity. They compare their own behaviors to that of their dads' and say to themselves, *I'm not bad, because I don't hit as hard (don't hit at all, don't yell as loud, don't scream with the same intensity) as my father.* However, those are relative statements and while one may not engage in physical violence, there may be controlling behavior by way of yelling, shouting, put-downs or withholding affection or money. In other instances, some men who were exposed to abusive fathers may seek to be the exact opposite. These men may walk away or avoid conflict altogether with the result being that nothing gets resolved. Their partners are left feeling abandoned and unsatisfied in the face of unresolved matters.

Consider the pendulum: It swings both ways. The behavior of your parent may have been far out there. You may have brought the pendulum down a notch and by comparison feel that's enough when, in reality, the issue is still harmful. Remember the analogies of the patient who smoked and the hole in the boat. Over time a negative or bad behavior can still ruin a marriage. That your behavior is not as frequent, intense or lasting as what you were exposed to in your childhood doesn't mean it is without effect. Further, the pendulum can swing so far the other way that different problems are created, such as withdrawal and avoidance. The challenge in marriage rescue is to have a pendulum that hangs true, neither too much to one side nor to the other.

LOOK AT YOURSELF

Given our reflection thus far on each partner taking responsibility, in order to rescue your marriage the first step is to examine the mantra: It's not me; it's you.

Ask yourself, *What am I doing that may be contributing to the problem?* Here are some questions to consider during your self-reflection:

- Are you too submissive, controlling, demanding, acquiescing, dependent or independent?
- Are you able to speak your mind?

- Do you listen?
- Do you treat each joint decision as a contest to be won?
- Are you able to separate your needs from that of your partner and advance the needs of your partner over your own?
- Are you able to assert yourself and let your needs and wants be known in a manner that takes nothing away from your partner?
- Are you and your partner able to prioritize each other so that you are suitably available to each other?
- Do you have any habits that are harmful to yourself or anyone else?
- Do you have any traits or behaviors that are irritating to your partner?
- Do you share in household chores?
- Do you clean up after yourself?
- Are you obsessed with neatness, such that your partner can never meet your standards?
- Do you make financial decisions jointly?
- Do you believe that only your way is the right way?
- Do you have healthy boundaries?
- Are you able to agree on rules with respect to visits from family and friends?
- Are you a pushover?
- Are you a bully?
- Do you use foul language with your partner?
- Do you remember your manners?
- Are your parenting strategies appropriate?
- Do you spend time with your children?
- Do you spend too much time with your children and not enough time with your partner?
- Are you and your partner on the same page sexually?

- Are you independent of your family of origin?
- Are you able or willing to participate in recreational activities that are of interest to your partner?
- Do you spend more time blaming and less time self-examining?

This list of questions is not exhaustive of all the issues that you may bring to your relationship. If you have recognized an issue (or issues) in yourself, then like the boat with a slow leak, you may be sinking your marriage. You will have to address the issue(s) within yourself if you want to have the kind of marriage that is sustainable and fulfilling.

ERIKSON AND THE STAGES OF ADULTHOOD

It is important to consider the kind of marriage you want for the rest of your life and, in particular, you want to think about the kind of marriage you will have at the very end of life.

The theories of Erik Erikson, a German-born psychologist, can be found in almost every introductory psychology textbook. Erikson was a developmental psychologist who took a view of human development from birth unto death. Prior to Erikson, many developmental psychologists focused on childhood and viewed all of adulthood as a single achievement. Erikson determined that adulthood is marked by several stages. Most important for our discussion is the final stage of human life that Erikson talked about: integrity versus despair.

Erikson helps us to understand that, in the final stage of life, people typically reflect on their lives and try to make sense of them. Imagine lying on your deathbed, reflecting back, trying to figure out how you feel about your life. Imagine holding in your hands a ledger, an accounting of all your life's deeds. In the ledger are only two columns: The column on the right lists all the things about which you feel good. The column on the left lists all the things about which you feel bad or regret. There is no more time for ledger entries. There is only time to tally the columns.

At the end of life and with ledger in hand, all we can do is calculate the outcome. If the tally of things about which we feel good is greater than the tally of things about which we feel bad then we greet death with a sense of integrity, a good feeling about ourselves and our lives. However, if the tally of things about which we feel bad is greater than the tally of things about which we feel good then we confront death filled with despair, a bad feeling about ourselves and our lives. The objective at the end of life is to face death with integrity.

Modern psychology has taught us that this stage of life is universal. Regardless of one's culture or race, no one is exempt from the process of examining one's life as one approaches its end. What's important to remember is that at this stage of life, all you can do is balance the columns. It's too late for anything more. It is imperative to understand that the entries into your journal of life are based upon every decision, interaction, behavior and choice you make every moment between now and the time you lay on your deathbed.

I'm reminded of visiting my Aunt Esther on her deathbed when she was ninety-two years of age. My wife and I last saw her in the final stages of cancer. It was only a matter of days before her passing. Seated beside her, I watched her eyes slowly open and close with each breath. I took Aunt Esther's arthritis-gnarled hand in mine and asked her to tell me a story. "What story can I tell you?" she asked.

"Tell me a story about the best day in your life." She replied that would be easy; she would tell me about Sunday, just a few days prior to my visit. I joked with her, "Aunt Esther, at ninety-two, you have a lot of days to choose from. What on earth would make this past Sunday the best day in your life?"

Aunt Esther explained that on the previous Sunday almost all of her family had been present for a visit. Aunt Esther was the eldest of six siblings. All her brothers and sisters had come to her bedside. Of their remaining spouses, all were present. Although Aunt Esther had lost a son many years ago, her other son and his wife were present too. Also there were Aunt Esther's husband and all of her grand-children and great-grandchildren.

I understood. As Aunt Esther lay on her deathbed, the matriarch of her family, she had all around her the people who were most dear in her life. With a seventy-year marriage intact, she was set to pass on with integrity. In the end, the real end, it was her relationships that mattered most. Her ledger was balanced toward the good.

As I've indicated, it is so often the case that when a marriage is in distress the partners are pointing fingers at each other. *It's not me; it's you.*

Integrity is not found in blame. It is found in introspection and accepting accountability for one's contribution to distress. Finding fault in others is easy. The hard work is in examining one's self and taking responsibility for what one finds—the good and the bad. While most couples in therapy can enumerate the faults of their partners, I turn things around so individuals can examine the issues they bring to their relationships that create dysfunction. Only by taking responsibility for one's personal contribution to distress will things ever change for the better. If each spouse simply blames the other, the vicious cycle contin-ues, unremitting. We only have control of ourselves and cannot com-pel anyone else to do something he or she is unprepared to do. As we change our own behaviors, however, we set the stage for our spouses to change. When we no longer blame our partners, we have already altered the dynamic of conflict and allow for the possibility of resolution.

June's Story

June, a woman who wanted advice, called me on the phone. She sought counseling for her husband. She warned that her husband had an anger management problem and abused alcohol, a habit that had been going on for many years. June stated that her husband blamed her for all of his prob-lems. She went on to tell me that she was confused and she begged me to see her spouse for a counseling session. June also asked what she could do differently to make her husband happy.

I told June that while it was not unreasonable to take issue with her partner's intolerable problems, she was asking all the wrong questions. There was a part of their marital distress that was about her and not about him, but she was missing it. The real concern and the part she brought to the discussion that contributed to her distress was her vulnerability.

I advised June to seek counseling for herself, possibly on site at a local women's shelter, not with a view to learning what would make her partner happy, but with a view toward exploring her own vulnerability such that she would fall prey to an abusive alcoholic. I discussed with her that her vulnerability inadvertently contributed to her partner's abuse of her.

If she wanted things to change, she needed to shore up her defenses and learn to take care of herself so that she could either stand up to her partner or take other action, such as ending the relationship. She would have to examine her vulnerability in the context of her partner's abusive behavior to ensure her safety for whatever she decided, but change rested on her taking action by addressing her vulnerability.

This may not be a salvageable relationship. However, for it to be salvageable this woman had to learn to manage her vulnerability, set expectations for reasonable behavior directed at her and maintain a boundary with respect to those expectations. She would also have to learn how to keep herself safe in the event her husband continued his abusive ways. If she was able to do that, she might be able to enjoy or develop a non-exploitative relationship. She might not fall prey to anyone like her husband again. She would probably need considerable support in this endeavor, but this was her task to improve herself and, by extension, her situation.

IT'S NOT ME; IT'S YOU

Typically when spouses enter into counseling, each tries his or her best to convince the counselor that even if he or she does have some minor issues, the real problems undermining the relationship are attributable to the other partner.

The role of the counselor in this situation is to help each person more realistically appraise his or her own contribution to distress. Though the contribution may not be equal between the partners, the challenge is to look inward. Further, the role of the counselor is to unbalance the status quo so that new behaviors may take place. After shaking spouses out of their complacency, out of the usual view of things, counselors can then guide spouses to reorganize around a new understanding, thus dealing with each other differently and better.

For couples who want to rescue marriages in distress, they have to understand the meaning of the term *crazy* as it relates to conflicted marital relationships. The simplest way to define *crazy* in this circumstance is doing the same thing over and over again and expecting a different result. So when we examine *it's not me; it's you*, this practice has to change. Ask yourself, *What is it about me that initiates, contributes to or perpetuates our marital problems?* Whatever that is has to change.

TAKING RESPONSIBILITY FOR ONESELF

This is not a matter of who goes first but of taking responsibility for oneself. It is always the right time and the mature thing to accept accountability. Taking responsibility for oneself leads to a life of integrity. Let's look at the marital turmoil of Darrel and his wife, Sara.

Darrel and Sara's Story

Darrel had always complained nastily about his wife, Sara. He complained that Sara didn't get things done around the house and couldn't look after the children. According to Darrel, Sara just didn't do anything well enough to meet his expectations. Sara felt worse and worse about herself. She became depressed and began taking a medication prescribed by her doctor, but nothing improved. Try as she might, she could never satisfy Darrel.

Indeed, from Darrel's point of view, it looked as if all their marital issues had to do with his wife.

Sara went back to see her medical doctor, because the medication for her depression didn't seem to be making a difference. The doctor took a few minutes to explore Sara's marriage and learned from her that she felt she could never measure up to her husband's expectations. The doctor recommended marital therapy.

Darrel was willing and agreed to go to marital therapy, thinking it would help reform his wife. He thought he could register his complaints about Sara and the therapist would help her change so they could get on with their marriage.

In marital therapy Darrel learned that although he was not as abusive as his father had been when Darrel was a child, he was still abusive to his wife. The therapist helped Darrel to see that he had attitudes similar to his father's. Though not as severe, these attitudes were affecting his wife and his relationship with her. What was, in Darrel's mind, supposed to be an exposé of his wife turned out to be a critical look at himself.

Sara too required self-reflection on her behaviors in their marriage. She discovered she had to learn to express herself and be less accepting of Darrel's unreasonable expectations and criticisms. She had to set her own expectations. For his part, Darrel had to learn to accommodate. Darrel wasn't an inherently bad man and once he recognized his contribution to distress, he took responsibility and changed. He had come to learn he couldn't just blame his wife and make it look like it was all her fault.

Daryl learned that *it's not me; it's you* is a lie. It's a myth we propagate to lay blame on another, to distance ourselves from our own issues to avoid responsibility. In the next chapters we will examine the other lies, myths and stories we tell ourselves that perpetuate marital distress. By examining these myths we will learn new things about ourselves so we can change our own behavior, the behavior that contributes to the distress of our partners.

You are welcome to your feelings, but the success or failure of your marriage lies in what you do versus what you feel. You can be angry or sad, but you will have to manage your feelings such that they do not inappropriately intrude on your partner. Having a feeling doesn't give anyone the right to act upon it and give grief to another. You need to manage your feelings responsibly. What you do will determine how you are received by others, more so than how you feel. There will be no more doing the same thing over and over again and expecting a different result. A different result requires different behavior. It starts with declaring, "Here's what I do that contributes to distress and co-creates marital turmoil. Here's what I am going to change to address my contribution to our marital distress, whether or not you do anything!"

The Winner's Motto:
I take responsibility for my behavior
and avoid blaming my partner.

Letting the In-Laws Interfere

The Sinner's Motto:
Why can't my mom hang around?

In the movie *My Big Fat Greek Wedding*, Toula's family members can't resist commenting on and intruding upon her life. They are loud and obnoxious, though loving. Meanwhile, Toula's fiancé, Ian, is from a more disengaged, quiet, Anglo Saxon Protestant family. While Ian is, at times, overwhelmed by Toula's family, he often finds it appealing and appreciates the warmth they exude. However, if we were to check in with him a few years later, what was once appealing likely now feels smothering. He is probably miserable about his lack of privacy, ready to get rid of her parents somehow and desperate for some alone time.

The real issue here is boundaries: how and where to set them and how to maintain them. With respect to boundaries, it's important to understand why some people let their parents intrude or violate limits.

UNMET NEEDS

Some grown children are still looking for love, adoration and validation from their parents. They have unmet emotional needs. These grown children willingly let their parents intrude in their lives, hoping that it will somehow appease their parents and thus have their own unmet needs finally satisfied. In other instances, these adults may have been and still are being indulged or taken care of by their parents and see nothing wrong with that, apart from the distress of their spouses. In this circumstance, an adult continues to enjoy being coddled by his or her parents and is used to this as his or her way of life. In reality, these adults are spoiled and child-like, because their parents continue to treat them as children, despite the fact that they are now adults.

What creates an unmet need? Imagine a child whose mother or father was not emotionally available while he or she was growing up. Maybe a parent was a workaholic; maybe a single parent was less available due to long work schedules; maybe there was violence in the home that distracted the parents from the care of the child and caused the child to experience fear; maybe one parent suffered a mental illness that interfered in that parent's availability to the child; maybe a parent was abusive, neglectful or exploitative when his or her needs and wants took priority over the child's needs and wants; maybe one parent was involved in drugs or alcohol or was engaged in an extramarital relationship. In all these ways a parent is not able to provide the love and care necessary for a child to feel whole and complete about him or herself.

Consider the plight of Margaret, a mother of two young children.

Margaret and Martin's Story

Margaret's husband, Martin, was furious, because Margaret's mother was always imposing on Margaret to run errands for her.

Margaret's father was an alcoholic and her mother didn't want to ask him to run errands for fear of him drinking and driving. Margaret's mother had never confronted her husband about his drinking, instead preferring to act as if all was well, even though Margaret, her only child, was inconvenienced.

During Margaret's childhood, her mother was depressed due to her husband's alcohol abuse and she was not emotionally available to Margaret. Now Margaret felt beholden to her mother, recognizing the difficult life her mother had with her father. Further, Margaret secretly wished to be adored, appreciated and validated by her mother and so she continually made herself available in hopes that her mother would finally give her that sense of love and care.

Martin, in turn, had to pick up the slack when Margaret was trotting off to appease her mother. Martin viewed Margaret's mother as manipulative, because she made Margaret feel guilty when Margaret didn't do as requested. He felt that Margaret always had to compensate for her father's alcoholism and that when she didn't, Margaret's mother made Margaret feel like an inconsiderate daughter.

Martin had had it with both of Margaret's parents and he kept telling Margaret to ignore her mother and pay more attention to their two young children.

EMOTIONAL VOIDS

It is not uncommon for children who grew up in circumstances similar to Margaret's to continue to seek the adoration and validation from their parents that they missed in childhood. It is the love and

validation that one receives as a child that contributes to the positive sense of self we refer to as self-esteem, so critical to adult func-
tioning, including social relationships. This is so crucial that if one
doesn't experience it with one's parents as a child, one's adult life can
be deeply affected, like Margaret's. For some, this effect shows up
as depression and/or anxiety. For others, they may forever feel the
need to seek their parents' validation. Because of this, they volun-
tarily subordinate their own needs to the intrusions or exploitations
of their parents in the secret hope that this will eventually win their
parents' affection and finally quench their thirst for parental love and
validation.

Given that some people have emotional voids they are seeking
to fill, they can be remarkably vulnerable to the demands of their
parents. This can occur even when the behavior of the parents is bla-
tantly obvious and intentionally negative. The challenge for a person
in this situation to set a boundary is overcoming the fear that if he
or she is successful, the parent may reject the adult child. This person
fears he or she may forever lose the perceived opportunity for feeling
loved by the parent in the way the child has been seeking. The thought
of never attaining parents' love and validation can cause an adult to
feel incomplete and worthless as a person. This person secretly wor-
ries, *If my own parent cannot tell me I am loved and lovable, then how can
I be valued by anyone?*

Being married to a person with an emotional void can be a
remarkable challenge. The spouse of such a person will likely advise
his or her partner about how abusive, self-centered, exploitative or
narcissistic the parent is. In reply, the spouse will defend the parent,
will excuse any inappropriate behavior and will ultimately expect the
parent to be accepted on the basis of being family. There will be an
assumption that the other spouse must tolerate the parent's inappropriate behavior.

The truth is this person is not defending his or her parent but
rather his or her own sense of self. He or she is seeking to protect
him or herself from profound feelings of worthlessness. Attacking the

family attacks the fantasy of one day feeling complete and worthy. Protection of the parent(s) is actually self-protection.

Marriages affected by these family dynamics have one spouse who continually runs to meet the needs of his or her parents ahead of the needs of the other partner and even those of the children, whose well-being may be put at risk in the quest for parental adoration and validation. For example, a spouse may let his or her alcoholic parent provide babysitting services even if that alcoholic parent may be intoxicated at the time of caring for the children. Or the spouse may let his or her parent care for the children knowing that the parent may say bad things about the spouse, causing a rift between the children and their parent. These spouses will not withhold the children and tell their parents they are not fit to care for the grandchildren. They are afraid of upsetting their own parents and losing any chance of being loved appropriately. It is as if these people are offering up their children to less than adequate care hoping to gain their parents' approval.

The children are put at risk so that the affected parent might gain love and validation never previously obtained. The spouse's priorities are inadvertently skewed as he or she maximizes the risk to the children in favor of gaining a chance of receiving love from a parent. The likelihood of finally receiving one's validation by allowing undesirable behavior to continue is too remote to contemplate reasonably. Unfortunately, a person in this situation is so fragile from not having had childhood emotional needs met that he or she will do anything for the chance to feel loved.

These circumstances are often enough to make the other partner feel miserable, frustrated and angry. The partner will likely not want the children exposed to risk or the inappropriate comments, behavior or intoxication of the grandparent. However, the adult child of these inappropriate parents may be so emotionally insecure that he or she will grossly minimize or deny the inherent risks or impropriety of his or her parents' care of the children, harboring the secret wish that this will endear him or her to the parents or, at the very least, minimize the risk of estrangement from them.

These are very powerful forces. The solution to this dilemma will never be found in berating your spouse's parents, though. Berating will cause your spouse to be more emotionally insecure and this will only serve to drive your spouse closer to his or her parents. Berating or belittling will entrench your spouse in defending his or her parents.

What you have to understand is that your spouse hasn't yet emotionally separated from his or her parents, because his or her emotional needs are as yet unmet. To separate from his or her parents will cause your spouse to feel like he or she will never be a complete person; that the void will never be filled; that he or she will forever feel worthless. Confronted with the threat of emotionally separating from his or her parents by force, your spouse will feel at times depressed and at other times anxious. If you pursue this separation, you will be viewed as demanding and controlling. As this dynamic continues, your spouse will seem increasingly anxious and you will appear increasingly controlling and abusive. Your behavior, aimed at liberating your spouse, will be your spouse's excuse for continuing the current relationship with his or her parents. While you may be good at assessing the dynamics between your spouse and your spouse's parents, remember, you must also examine your own behavior.

DISCUSSION OF MARGARET AND MARTIN

A challenge for both Margaret and Martin is appreciating the role Margaret plays in her parents' dynamic. She is her mother's savior and is self-protective at the same time. Margaret keeps herself and her mother from confronting her father's drinking. Further, when her father is unavailable, Margaret fulfills her mother's needs as a spousal substitute. Rather than either of them challenging Margaret's father about his drinking, mother and daughter have developed their own structure so that Margaret is responsible for her mother's care, likely an extension of a dynamic borne from Margaret's early childhood. Margaret is keen to jump into the void with the hope that it brings her closer to winning her mother's love and validation.

To get Margaret's mother out of Margaret's marriage, several things need to occur: her father's drinking has to be addressed; her mom has to learn to access other services; Margaret has to learn to set boundaries with her mother; Martin has to learn to be supportive of Margaret in view of her challenges.

A challenge for Margaret, who wants to fulfill her perceived obligations, is to confront her parents about their problematic relationship and get herself out from between them. Perhaps the biggest challenge will be addressing how Margaret feels about herself, especially as she potentially betrays her mother and possibly loses her chance for her father's affection. She will wrestle with feelings of fear of abandonment as punishment for addressing her father's alcoholism and thus never receiving the love she believes she needs to feel whole as a person. She fears her betrayal will seal her terrible fate as an unworthy person.

If Margaret's father isn't abusive and his only problem is with alcohol, Margaret needs to talk with him and explain how his drinking affects her life and her mother's. With her mother she has to discuss how she feels that her life has been on hold, running to address her mother's needs ahead of her own and following through because she has never felt fully loved and validated. Margaret will need to risk her parents' wrath at her exposing the dysfunctional family dynamic and, indeed, she may never receive the validation and appropriate care she's sought. This is the plight of becoming an adult—emotionally separating from one's parents and becoming independent.

As Margaret takes on the task of addressing the family dynamic, she will no longer be subordinating herself to her parents hoping to be valued. She will be standing up for herself, acting in a way that suggests she values herself. That is the secret to reclaiming oneself and managing one's self-esteem and worth. Investing in oneself and not letting oneself be bullied or exploited is the antidote to emotional abuse or neglect and the tonic to vitalize one's sense of self-worth.

Margaret doesn't really need to address those issues with her parents but she can act as if she has. As a result of a new understanding of the dynamic in which she is embedded, she can respond differently, no longer viewing herself as beholden to her parents' demands and dysfunction. She can start to say no without reservation. When the onslaught of protests and manipulations occurs, she can recognize her parents' shortcomings for what they are, stand her ground and feel good about her investment in herself, children and family.

She can emotionally separate and limit her mother's intrusions and the effect of both her parents upon her. Their issues shall remain their issues and no longer be passed onto Margaret for her to be burdened by them. Margaret can feel buoyed by the realization that her separation from the parental dynamic will serve her own children, as they will not be subjected to the inappropriate role models of her parents or her own lack of emotional availability due to being distracted by her parents' issues.

As for Martin, instead of berating Margaret over her parents' issues befalling her, he needs to support Margaret in speaking with her father and mother. If Margaret does talk with her parents, the challenge for Martin is not to take over and carry out the task for her, but to understand that this is a frightening situation for Margaret and act as a support in her endeavor with her parents. Margaret must experience Martin's support or else she will feel at risk of abandonment by her parents with no emotional safety net. Margaret must feel that Martin is her emotional anchor and not a predator ready to pounce should she falter.

If Margaret chooses not to talk with her parents but to go straight to setting boundaries, that's okay. In either case, Martin needs to be his wife's cheerleader. Martin may need to increase his demonstrations of affection. Margaret will likely crave hugs and want to be held and to feel secure. Martin may never have been a physically affectionate person; instead he may be the kind of person who only complains when things are not going right. If that is the case, his lack of emotional expression would only fuel Margaret's need to continue to seek affection from her parents.

Martin's role is crucial. He too may have to make significant efforts to engage in new and perhaps previously uncomfortable behavior to help his wife feel worthy and validated as a spouse and parent. It is not enough to bring home his paycheck, cut the lawn and take out the garbage. While these are good instrumental displays of caring, Martin must also use words and gestures. He must tell his wife directly that he loves and adores her and that he appreciates her efforts and the things she does on his behalf. It is reasonable to thank your spouse for the everyday things he or she does and to compliment him or her. It is necessary to use manners and say please, thank you and you're welcome. These are the behaviors that signal to others that they are of value. Nothing is left to chance, because if unsaid or unde-monstrated, doubt creeps in like a terrible cancer.

The real challenge in keeping Margaret's mother from interfering in their lives is in appreciating what is at stake emotionally for Margaret. Until that is addressed, nothing will change. The challenge for Martin, again, is not to berate Margaret, as that will only encour-age her to seek from her mother the validation she craves, bringing her mother more in between her and Martin. Martin has to be patient and be a source of support, safety and validation. That is where coun-seling can be important. When spouses cannot agree or see the dynamics in which they are entrenched, counseling can help to gain perspective and then solutions are more readily visible.

Margaret never did confront her parents, but as a result of attending counseling with Martin, they both gained perspective.

Martin learned strategies to demonstrate more support and emotional expressiveness. This was a challenge for Martin, who was somewhat immature in terms of his ability to be affectionate, but with the therapist's support, he was able to make positive changes. He began to give his wife hugs and ask about her day.

Margaret began limiting her responses to her mother's demands. Over time, Margaret's mother realized that she was no longer effective at eliciting her daughter's care, particularly when it interfered with Margaret meeting her own needs and those of her family. Her mother stopped asking so much of Margaret, perhaps realizing Margaret had moved on with her own life and family obligations. Martin, at the same time, was able to express his appreciation and not take this for granted.

Tony and Maria have different problems and issues with their in-laws:

Tony and Maria's Story

Tony's parents were immigrants with a traditional marriage. Theirs was a good marriage as everyone knew their places and everyone worked within their roles' boundaries and definitions.

Tony's mother did everything for him. Tony never had to lift a finger but he also respected his mother, who quickly and easily gave Tony a spank with the wooden spoon if he ever got out of line when he was a child. Clearly, she was the master of the home.

Maria, while of the same cultural background as Tony, had a family that operated differently from Tony's. Her parents had a good marriage, but her parents' roles were more elastic; her parents could stretch out of their roles and do things more typical of the opposite gender. Her father often helped out in the home, cooking and cleaning, and her mother worked outside the home.

Maria learned to be flexible, independent and self-reliant. Because her mother worked outside the home, Maria learned to fend for herself and do her own laundry. Because of her father's role inside the house, she was used to him participating in household chores and came to view this as a family norm. Her parents expected and respected that people could do things for themselves as well as for each other.

When Tony and Maria were dating, Maria appreciated and enjoyed the attention she received from Tony's mother. Maria felt catered to and experienced this behavior lovingly. After their wedding, however, Tony's mother extended her care from her own home to that of Tony and Maria's home.

While Maria and Tony were on their honeymoon, Tony's mother entered their home and rearranged the kitchen cupboards, stocked the refrigerator, made their bed and even rearranged the supplies in the bathroom. His mother thought Tony would be happy. Now Maria and Tony's home was just like Tony's home when he left it for his marriage.

When Tony and Maria arrived home from their honeymoon, Tony felt a kind of comfort, sensing a familiarity within his home. Maria felt a sense of intrusion and was fearful their house had been invaded and belongings perhaps stolen. Nothing was missing, however; yet nothing was the same. Minutes after Tony and Maria returned home, Tony's parents entered with warm hugs, well wishes and food.

Tony's mother had treated Tony and Maria's home as an extension of her own and rearranged the furniture and Maria and Tony's things. Maria, raised to be independent, to take care of herself and to rely on a husband to share in chores, realized that she was now to be the child of Tony's mother and her role within her own house would be determined by her mother-in-law. Feeling sick, Maria stayed in the bathroom until Tony's parents left.

Tony was oblivious to Maria's feelings. She felt she could hardly contain them. She washed her face with cool water and then rearranged the bathroom the way she liked it. Then she exited, deciding to confront Tony.

Maria couldn't contain her rage and barraged Tony about his mother's intrusiveness and disrespect for her privacy. Tony, having absolutely no appreciation of the issue, attributed Maria's rage to jet lag.

Arguments continued for the next several days, long enough for Tony to realize Maria really did have an issue with his mother. However, from his perspective, he only experienced his mother as caring and, for the entirety of his life, enjoyed the services she provided. He had also learned as a child that as long as he went along with his mother's wishes he was not reprimanded and was not given chores. For him, lack of privacy and little independence was a small price to pay for keeping his mother happy and eluding her wrath.

Tony and Maria had dated for four years prior to marriage. They got along great and although Maria knew Tony's mother did everything for him, it really wasn't an issue and she couldn't have anticipated that his mother would extend her reach into their house. Tony and Maria hadn't encountered any problems in their relationship until they returned home from their honeymoon.

MARITAL ADJUSTMENT

Tony and Maria are spouses who have a lot to work on to adjust to marital life. Never having had to deal with conflict before, they need to learn to deal with challenges, set boundaries and determine their respective roles as husband and wife. Most of all, either Tony needs to address their need for independence and privacy with his mother or Maria needs to learn to accept her mother-in-law's behavior.

However, Maria is most likely never going to accept or adjust to this circumstance. Tony will have to make some significant adjustments. Marital issues aren't always split evenly between two partners. Sometimes one has to change more than the other does.

The challenge for Tony is explaining to his mother that, while they appreciate her desire to help, when it is unsolicited it interferes with him and Maria forming their own family and way of doing things. He must do this in such a way that his mother will not perceive Maria to be unappreciative of his mother's support. Therefore, these remarks must come from Tony with Tony asserting himself as the master of his domain, now independent from his parents' home.

Tony must not reject or disrespect his mother but establish himself as setting the rules with his wife for their own home. No more fear of wooden spoons. He is an adult with the rights and privileges accorded to any adult. His mother can continue to care for his father and, upon request, can do favors for Tony and Maria, for which they will be appreciative. Tony must assert that he wants his wife to be the queen in her domain, as his mother is in hers; that this is how he respects his wife and her role within their home; that just as no one can tell his mother or his father how to do things in their own home, no one can tell Tony and Maria how to do things in their home.

In addition to Tony speaking with his mother, Tony and Maria must talk. They need to determine how the household chores will be shared between them. It may be that Tony never lifted a finger in his parents' home, so he may have some learning to do. Assuming a willing attitude, these matters can be settled quickly. If, however, one partner takes exception to sharing chores or doesn't fulfill his or her end of the bargain, strife will reign and sex will quickly fall away. Left unresolved, a couple such as Tony and Maria will be seen as him being a mama's boy and her being a bitch.

Here is a suggested strategy for Tony's face-to-face conversation with his mother:

Mom, I want to thank you for all the things you have done for me growing up. You have taken care of me and helped me to become a man. I am married now and have become the man of my own home with my wife, Maria. It's time for us to learn to do things on our own and in our own way.

While I appreciate your willingness to continue to be helpful, at this point it stops me from being an independent adult and it stops me and my wife from being masters in our own house. While I appreciate all that you have done for us, it is time to stop. We have to find our own way.

One day, you and dad will not be here to do things for us. Better we learn now when we are still young and able to learn ourselves. If we ever need help or support, we would like to think we can still turn to you for guidance and a helping hand. We would be most grateful for that. It would provide us a sense of comfort knowing you are there as our safety net if things get tough and we need help.

I love you and we are looking forward to having you over to enjoy our home and our meals when invited and we will enjoy coming over to your home when invited. If we ever just want to drop by, we will call first to make sure you are home and the *timing is okay for you. Similarly, if you want to drop by, please give us a call first to make sure we are home and the timing is agreeable.*

I am so pleased you raised me to be a respectful man and I appreciate that you will respect my wishes on this so I can now make my family for Maria and me, the way you made your family for you and dad.

After Tony has his talk with his mother and as Tony learns and takes on new chores, it is important for Maria to express appreciation. It is never acceptable for a spouse to take it for granted that the other partner knows what to do or how to do it, particularly when never done before. For Tony, this is a remarkably new way of life. He is behaving unconventionally, as far as he is concerned, and a little appreciation would make him feel like his efforts are worthwhile.

If Tony addresses this issue now and discusses with Maria how they will manage household chores and finances together, then they are on their way to making a lasting marriage.

The Winner's Motto:
It's up to me to set boundaries with my parents.

Putting Your Friends
Ahead of Your Partner

The Sinner's Motto:
What's wrong with my friends?

What works for single life may not work for married life. Things change and friends may need to change to suit a new lifestyle. While playing hockey with the boys twice a week and coming home late after drinking a few beers might be his idea of having fun, being stuck at home isn't her idea of having fun. Similarly, it's hard for him to get excited about her manicures and pedicures with the girls when he is concerned about the bills and worried about the gossip that he may be the brunt of when she registers her marital discontent with her friends.

Your friends might be important to you, but are they important to your partner? Can you conceive of *our* friends versus *my* friends? Do you have friends? Or are you so dependent on your partner that you can't do anything on your own and your partner feels stuck with you? "If you loved me, you wouldn't need anybody else." "Yeah, but if you loved me, I would be able to have some time with my friends." This is a setup for conflict. Where does the issue come from and what can you do about it? It starts with childhood.

Prior to adolescence one's friends are based on proximity: the kid next door, peers in extracurricular activities, teammates. Adolescence brings more personal mobility. One's circle of friends extends and one uses that circle of friends as the stepping-stones to separate eventually from one's family of origin. Friends begin to feel more important than family. Whereas the influence of one's parents was once paramount, now friends figure more measurably into one's thoughts, feelings and even decisions. They become everything and during adolescence, when emotions run high, those relationships are fraught with intensity.

The intensity is also fueled by the adolescent brain, a conglomerate of neurons, not yet fully formed or informed by life experience. As such, the adolescent brain does not yet understand the nature of risk, giving way to teenaged behavior that is inherently risky. So here are the makings of the basic teenager: the human animal seeking to extend its social territory in packs of like-minded animals who, as of yet, do not fully know the dangers in which they engage. This combination of factors is the proving ground for the development of intense relationships. There will be shared experiences based upon intensity of emotion as well as risky circumstances. While most adolescents survive this time of life, not all do. From ancient history to our era, those who don't survive teach by tragic example. Knowledge of them serves to modulate adolescents' behavior and develop their maturing brains, as seen in this story:

The young caveman, seeking to show off his prowess with the animals, exited the cave to poke the saber-toothed kitten while his mates looked on. In his fun and glory, neither he nor any of his companions noticed the mother saber-toothed tiger coming from behind. Protecting her kitten, the mother tiger pounced on the young caveman, ripping him to shreds. Lesson learned by the horrified onlookers.

As they mourned the death of their friend and felt more united by their shared intense experience, they came to understand: don't upset the wildlife and life is fragile. They provided each other comfort and they left their adolescent ways behind, now wiser, less prone to taking risks and with a remarkable sense of camaraderie. They were important to each other.

Through this process of shared intense emotional experiences, we bond very closely with our friends and, as we do, these very same friends form the means that allow us to move from our families of origin into the greater world of other relationships.

Pete and Frank's Story

When Pete was eight, he and a neighborhood boy named Frank were inseparable. They ran in their yards, biked the conservation area, waded the streams. Then came soccer and they were on separate teams. Their time together as friends was limited, but they still talked with each other most days after school. In high school their separate interests, music versus sports, took them in yet further directions. They each developed a group of friends and while they remained friends themselves on one level, they had very little actual time together.

When Pete was of driving age, he took to fast cars and he often could be seen under the hood making modifications before showing up at the local hangout where other teen car enthusiasts got together. Frank delved deeper into his music studies and he also enjoyed experimenting with drugs and alcohol. Frank had not only his rock band, but also his band of like-minded musician buddies who indulged in alcohol and drugs.

Eventually both Pete and Frank grew up enough to discover the wonder of girls. Pete's girlfriend, Jennifer, was a cheerleader, having spent her childhood in gymnastics and dance. Given her experience in gymnastics, she was used to intense physical experiences and so she took to Pete's fast, skillful driving even though at times she was frightened by his apparent recklessness. Pete believed he could handle his car through any situation.

Frank's girlfriend, Molly, had fewer extracurricular opportunities when she was growing up and had been more of a homebody before entering high school where she was introduced to a broader range of people her age. Molly, with limited life experience, really took to Frank's attention and happily engaged in drug use with him. She was turned on by the thrill of his music and the use of drugs to further intensify the experience. She found some degree of comfort limiting herself to Frank's company and his companions.

These relationships continued to develop and all the while the boys also enjoyed time with their like-minded buddies who encouraged Pete's interest in cars and dangerous driving and Frank's music and expanding drug use. Their girls weren't just along for the ride. Their participation encouraged the activities of their boyfriends.

Jennifer had a circle of girlfriends outside of her relationship with Pete. They prided themselves on their boyfriends and from time to time squabbled about various boys and consoled each other about relationships that took turns for the worse.

Molly's acquaintances outside of the circle with Frank were marginal. For her, Frank provided the only other social experience of significance beyond her family. Her relationship with Frank took on great importance to her as her sole source of escape from her family and entrance to adulthood. She molded herself to Frank's needs and wants. She was somewhat lost to his personality and lifestyle.

Occasionally, there were arguments in these relationships, when Pete's driving was too reckless, Frank's drug use too risky and when high school was coming to an end and decisions about life after high school were at the forefront.

As is normal for teenage romance, not all relationships survive. Adolescence is meant to be the testing ground to develop relationship skills, not necessarily to result in one lasting relationship. While a few high school romances may endure, most provide the learning experience to better manage the intimate relationships of young adulthood.

With all these shared and intense experiences, though, these friendships feel like the most important relationships anyone could ever have. It is unbelievable, at the time, that by the end of adolescence most of these relationships will change, that one will move from a child of one's parents to a person in the world supported by the very friends developed in the shared and intense age of adolescence. No wonder people strive to hold on to those relationships, given their importance as the path to the independence of young adulthood.

When we couldn't talk with our parents, our friends were there. Their guidance may have been misdirected, but their support was unwavering. These were indeed important people.

Pete died in a car crash before his twentieth birthday. Jennifer wasn't in the car at the time. She spent the majority of her young adult life commiserating with her girlfriends as well as providing moving testimonials about the importance of safe driving. Now in her thirties, she is struggling in a relationship with a man who doesn't appreciate her need to continue her lectures or her need to stay so connected with the girlfriends of her teenage years. Those girlfriends helped her through very tough times. She wants a partner but having and keeping a partner is fraught with many emotional challenges. Her girlfriends, though, have always been there for her.

Frank's attention to music and drugs was greater than his attention to Molly. She turned to other boys just prior to leaving Frank. Because she had been so involved with Frank, though, her circle of girlfriends was small and so her relationship with her new partner has taken on more significance than what otherwise might have been the case had she had other friends. As for Frank, he too is in another relationship, superficial in nature relative to his attention to his friends in the band—a band that never had a hit song, but still forms the most important object of his attention.

Adolescence sends people into adulthood on different trajectories. Some find that mating and learning the right boundaries between them, their partners and their friends outside the inner circle come easily; others develop overdependence on their partners, who may feel it is like a restriction; still others are unable to move past their circles of teenage buddies and this interferes with developing the kind of intimacy and primacy of relationship that can maintain the sanctity of an intimate partnership. Friendships form through many experiences and the intensity and importance of those friendships can intrude upon intimate relationships. Finding balance can be a challenge of too many or too few.

ADOLESCENCE AND EXPERIENCE

These intense interpersonal experiences do not have to be as dramatic as noted, but can be as simple as parties, sports, first loves, jealousies or summertime antics. The adolescent brain will provide the perceived intensity. The magic of adolescence is boys and girls thinking they invented having fun.

The challenge in forming and maintaining relationships is in adapting to each other. This occurs as teens move through adolescence into young adulthood where there is typically a focus on coupling—finding a mate. Human beings, like all animals, are born to recreate themselves. Finding a mate with whom to do so is a natural evolutionary process. Dating is the activity prior to making a formal commitment of joint living and facilitates finding the right mate. People date to attune themselves with each other or to determine the possibility of attuning or adapting to each other. If they learn that they cannot attune or adapt to each other, if they are not well suited, then they will move on to the next relationship, hopefully before settling into one that doesn't quite fit. We go through all of this to find the perfect mate.

Dating has its own stages. Partners form an interest or attraction and then an infatuation. As the infatuation wanes, partners develop a more realistic appraisal of each other, at which time they can more reasonably determine how well suited they are to each other. However, not all people do the work of determining goodness of fit through dating prior to entering a more formal relationship, whether marital or cohabiting. These people are then stuck grinding through a shaping process after the fact.

Who knows how well two people will get along when they couple during the intense phase of infatuation, when their judgment is diluted by animal attraction? The lure draws them in, but whether the fit is good takes more time to discover. They have to complete the dance to determine the chance of the relationship having longevity. Partners' relationships or lack thereof with friends beyond a significant other need to be sorted out after the infatuation phase of dating, once the intensity of the first attraction begins to wane. Running headlong into coupling during infatuation may leave one with buyer's remorse, wondering why one made the purchase after the wrapper is removed.

FIGURING OUT FRIENDS

Figuring out a partner's friends or attitude toward friends is just one of many issues that need sorting out before making a cohabiting commitment. Left to after the fact, it remains a risk to the relationship, waiting to see if two people are indeed compatible in this area or if

differences can be sorted out. While for some this may come naturally, for others, unspoken expectations and unresolved issues may
create hardships and conflicts. Partners must adapt or risk the end of
the relationship.

Pair two people together where one is immersed in a world of
friends and the other whose friendship extends only to his or her
beloved and the relationship is ripe for trouble. There is no good and
no bad person here. This is an equal opportunity problem and brings
us back to the first sin's motto: it's not me; it's you. To sort things
out, it is vital to keep the perspective that the issue is the difference
between the partners and not either person's particular viewpoint or
needs. The issue becomes the partners' ability to traverse the distance
between them and find a balance that works for them as a couple,
with neither being caused to feel bad or angry. Partners need to find
balance between too many friends and too few friends.

However, if a person blames or, worse, vilifies a partner for too
many or too few friends, the relationship sinks and starts to foul. As
one complains that the other partner is insecure and has no friends,
the other complains the first partner is insensitive to his or her needs
and detached. They argue and name-call back and forth like two young
children. What one partner considers normal, the other first calls bad
and then calls wrong.

This is what transpires from coupling too early and subverting
the dating process. Dating is important and should form a vital part
of any relationship. Try before you buy; this is not a sexual reference,
but a reference to getting to know a person well, long after the infatuation has worn off and you can make a realistic appraisal with regard
to how well you both get along and manage conflict and whether you
have mutual goals and aspirations.

OTHER PEOPLE AND INTIMATE RELATIONSHIPS

Intimate relationships require a balancing act between the time and
energy put toward being a couple versus the time and energy put

toward other people and interests. The time spent with other people or other interests shouldn't threaten the relationship. There must be an understanding that partners need time for both: time for the relationship and time for other people and things. What the right amount is will be different from couple to couple. That is why you cannot compare your relationship to others, lest others advise based on what fits for them rather than an appreciation of your uniqueness as a couple and as individuals. It is easy to find friends who support your point of view. You are very unlikely to turn to people who would challenge your point of view in favor of your partner's. Thus the counsel of loved ones or friends will likely be biased and, when brought into the situation of trying to settle things with your partner, will almost always do more to inflame the situation than resolve it.

If your relationship is in trouble because one of you is feeling smothered or one partner's friends seem to be of greater priority than the other partner, you must, as I've indicated from the beginning of this book, examine yourself first.

Ask yourself these questions: Apart from your intimate partner, do you have other friends? Do you see, talk or communicate with them? Do you have any interests that are independent of your primary relationship? Do you apply time toward cultivating those interests? Are you comfortable going out and meeting people or doing things on your own? Are you a homebody? Do you hold the opinion that your partner should be the only person with whom you should have to spend time? Are you a solitary individual and your partner a more outgoing, social person?

You must also examine your insecurities and where they might originate. Reflect on your parents' relationship and its influence as a role model for you and your relationship. Was there enough bonding to hold your parents' partnership together? Did they go in different directions?

DISENGAGED AND ENMESHED RELATIONSHIPS

When partners evolve in different directions and perhaps are not available emotionally for each other, it is a *disengaged* relationship.

Alternately, when partners are so entwined with each other that one feels smothered—unable to step away without the other seeming to crumble—they are in an *enmeshed* relationship. However, being too distant or too close is only a problem if it creates distress in you or your loved one. It is only inherently problematic if there isn't that goodness of fit, where both are comfortable with the situation.

Depending on what you discover in your self-examination, you may find you are indeed over-reliant upon your partner to fulfill all your needs. This can be a daunting and overwhelming task for anyone. In the beginning of your relationship, things may have been great. From your partner's perspective, he or she may have viewed your behavior not as dependence but as adoration and love. He or she may have seen you as keenly aware of his or her needs and may have been grateful for your attention. In the beginning of the relationship, when infatuation is normal and undivided attention common, your partner may have truly appreciated and enjoyed your over-reliance and overlooked it as something that could develop permanently or create an issue later on in the relationship.

As a relationship develops and matures, there is usually an expectation that partners loosen their exclusive grip on each other to include time for other friends, activities and interests. While it is normal at the beginning of a relationship to turn attention inward toward each other in order to determine the suitability and goodness of fit and to develop the kind of bonding that creates lasting care and affection, it is also normal that once the bond is made and seems to be secure, partners then attend to matters and interests beyond the immediacy of the relationship.

At this point in a relationship, partners can get back in touch with friends and activities of interest, all the while holding the intimate relationship special. However, if you are unable to move past the exclusivity that is a hallmark of the infatuation stage of coupling and your partner feels smothered or restricted, then your relationship may be regarded as enmeshed, a situation where you are trying to be constantly with your partner and there is an expectation that you and your partner feel and do everything together. Taken to the extreme, this enmeshment can be stifling and restrictive and can create the feeling that one partner needs to break loose from the other in order to maintain a separate sense of self. This often develops in children whose parents were enmeshed and did not allow for differentiation, eventual realistic individuation and independence.

Children of enmeshed families often have to rebel to escape from their parents' bind or alternately may submit, but this attachment often becomes symptomatic of anxiety or depression. Enmeshment can create mental health issues, both in partners and in children, when taken to levels beyond one's tolerance and where resolution is either hard fought or elusive. Remember, labeling, name-calling and seeking the validation of friends or family will not serve to resolve your marital distress. True self-exploration and responsibility will be necessary to resolve matters.

If you are insecure, if you have difficulty maintaining an independent self, if you feel emotionally abandoned, if you have an expectation that an intimate partnership should provide for all of each partner's needs, then the shift from the intensity of forming a special bond to returning one's attention to interests and matters outside of the special bond can feel like emotional abandonment. This can trigger concern for the loss of the relationship. In turn, this may cause you to feel the need to hold on even tighter to your partner and demand even more time together for fear of losing him or her to the temptations of the world outside your relationship.

You first expect, then request, then demand that your partner return home directly each evening from work, refrain from activities and friends and only attend to matters within your span of interest— typically on the home front. Meanwhile, your partner experiences your attitude or behavior as increasingly restrictive and, while at first accommodating, eventually comes to resent your expectations and demands. Your partner will then rebel by wrestling back independence against your wishes and expectations. Arguments predictably go back and forth as one partner wants too much attention and the other wants too much freedom. This continues until the relationship breaks under the strain. Resist blame, even when afraid, and examine

your situation from a broader perspective that keeps your contribution in full view.

Alternately, if you believe that your partner is spending too
much time with activities, interests or friends, that there is not sufficient time or energy directed to maintenance of the relationship and
you are upset, then your partner may be disengaged. You may feel
that, now established in the relationship, your partner is taking you
for granted, continuing to live life as set forth from the trajectory of
adolescence. You worry that your relationship may wither from lack
of attention. You wonder, *Why be with someone whose priorities seem so
distant to the relationship?* You worry that with your partner's attention elsewhere, it is only your insistence and work toward the relationship that keeps the semblance of a relationship intact.

Meanwhile, your partner views him or herself as a good friend
to others, whose availability makes him or her a wonderful person.
In the face of the great feelings that position generates, your partner
cannot fully understand your sense of loss for his or her availability.
If your partner cannot appreciate how or why you may need more
attention than that provided and why he or she cannot pursue interests and you feel that your partner is oblivious to your needs, and
your partner's only distress is your insistence on more time together
(which causes him or her to feel as if he or she must give up something), then you may be dealing with the impact of a relationship that
is disengaged. Note, however, that from your partner's perspective
and given your partner's life experience, this may be your partner's
"normal" and not felt to be a problem.

If you are the one whose partner is complaining about your lack
of availability, of feeling you are too distant or believing the relationship is undervalued as compared to your other interests, then you
are likely in distress, feeling thwarted in your fun, interests or other
important relationships. You cannot conceive that matters originating with yourself are contributing to your distress as a couple. You
resist your partner's projection of blame, thinking your partner insecure and restrictive. You may pathologize your partner and try to
convince him or her that that is where the problem resides and you

may cajole your partner to change so you can carry on as previously enjoyed. But as this continues, you may also see that it isn't resolving your troubles and, more likely, is exacerbating them. You too must remember the mistaken mantra of the first sin: it's not me; it's you.

If your partner is complaining that your friends come before your relationship and that you are not as available as your partner feels necessary for the relationship, ask yourself these key questions: Do you expect your partner to always wait for you? Are you frequently late returning home to your partner? Do you run to the needs of friends before checking with your partner first? Do you worry that if you aren't available to the requests or demands of others that they will think less of you; if so, is this difficult for you to manage? Are you afraid of letting down your friends? Might you be inadvertently over-responsive to your friends at the cost of your primary relationship?

If these questions resonate with you, you may indeed be relegating your relationship to low priority and creating resentment in your partner. Your partner probably feels left out and of less importance to you than your friends. Further, not making the effort for common decencies such as arriving on time, keeping in touch or advising of delays is distressing to anyone, let alone your partner. These behaviors are inherently disrespectful and disrespect is not conducive to a functional relationship. It may be very reasonable that your partner feels angry and disappointed, even if you are concerned with how your friends perceive you. In this situation, your need for recognition, acceptance and autonomy is greater than your ability to attend to a singular and special relationship.

Your partner is likely not as angry or dependent as you project, but is a victim of your inability to treat him or her with the same courtesy and respect as you do your friends and other interests. You may not be fully past the priorities of adolescence, ready to engage in a formal intimate relationship with a single partner. You may need a bit of a shove into adulthood to move past other lures and to concentrate on the task of forming and maintaining a singular, intimate adult relationship able to satisfy reasonable mutual needs.

BALANCING DISTANCE AND CLOSENESS

The difference between the partners' positions is what matters. The greater the difference, the more likely the conflict. However, the distance between the two sides is only one of the challenges for a couple struggling with these issues.

The willingness or ability of a person to take personal stock of oneself and responsibility for any contribution to distress without blaming someone else is essential to a good marriage. While the emotional distance between two people may be an issue, if one partner is stuck and unmovable with regard to his or her point of view, ascribing blame to the other partner and simply unwilling to change, then the outcome will be poor. Distance, degree of flexibility and willingness to take responsibility together will mark how surmountable your marital problems may be.

Both partners must take stock and look at respective beliefs, attitudes and needs. Think of your own family and your adolescence. Consider your connection to activities and friends over the course of your life. Maybe you need to move beyond yourself and the belief that your partner must be your absolute everything. While you may think that your beliefs, expectations and personal style work for you, in reality they don't. If they did, your relationship would not be in distress. It may be that for your relationship to work, you have to move out of your comfort zone and incorporate some changes to accommodate your partner. Your partner may be of a reasonable opinion about your issues and, at the same time, you may be of a reasonable opinion about your partner's. After mutual self-reflection, one partner may have to change more than the other, but likely both of you will have some changing to do to make the relationship more satisfying. As you argue less about these issues and make accommodations, conflict should diminish and mutual appreciation increase.

Who needs to change more doesn't matter. It's not about finding out who is worse or more in need of change. It is about the capability for mutual accommodation. Even if one's contribution to distress is small, remember that, over time, even a tiny hole can sink a ship.

SELF-EXAMINATION

Examine yourself. Seek help to do so if you are having difficulty.

Perhaps you will find you feel you need to monitor your partner because one of your parents had an affair and, to you, distance signals a concern for infidelity. Your relationship might have begun as an affair, so you worry that without supervision, your partner may drift again. Maybe your parents had a wonderful, close and loving relationship and complemented each other and you are only seeking to recreate this. Perhaps you are just not as outgoing as your partner and are more on the shy side. Whatever you discover about yourself that may be contributing to distress, address it, show some flexibility and adapt to improve your relationship. Improvement in the relationship will take mutual adaptations. You will have to learn new behavior and move beyond your present expectations and, very likely, beyond your comfort zone.

Similarly, in your self-examination you may find that your parents were two individuals whose love for each other was strong but whose need for closeness or proximity was not substantial, neither parent strayed and independence was reasonable to both. You may find that your parents were more comfortable as roommates than soulmates and you don't seek as much of an emotional or spiritual connection as you do a material or economic partnership. You may find you were so close to the friends of your youth that you cannot contemplate distancing from them. You may find you get so much enjoyment from your hobby or vocation that all else pales in comparison, including time with your partner.

Whatever you discover about yourself, it may need to change to facilitate the stability and satisfaction of your marriage. This is not about compromise but priorities. Compromise implies giving up something to get something else. The problem with that is that no one likes to give up anything. That is why I talk of prioritizing instead of compromising. If you set your marriage or relationship as the top priority, whatever you do in the pursuit of that priority is not a loss. You are gaining your first and most important objective: the relationship. This is always a win.

Sometimes it is more difficult for one person to accommodate than it is for the other. This may mean that one may have to examine what he or she seeks in a relationship against what the other partner can truly offer and determine if this is tolerable. In a relationship where for one partner dancing is enjoyable, is it tolerable if the other partner never learns to dance? Will the other good qualities of the relationship outweigh the loss of dancing with one's partner? Consider these questions: Will you be able to live within the limits of what your partner may be able to provide? Can you live with a good but not a great relationship? Can you live with adequate but not good? Can you adjust your expectations and needs? Can you find other ways to compensate for needs not met in the relationship that won't undermine the integrity of the partnership?

If you are keeping your partner close to the point that your partner is strained, perhaps you are too reliant on him or her or perhaps you have a reasonable concern that without your watchful eye, your partner may succumb to trouble. Either way this must be addressed. If there are some issues originating with your partner that are contributing to your need for greater closeness than is healthy for the relationship, then address it. You need to talk with your partner about your fears of your partner's behavior and develop strategies to manage more appropriately. If your need for closeness is more a function of your personality style, security needs or belief that your partner should provide for all your needs and wants, then you are going to have to move beyond that.

Depending on the problems, strategies to mitigate those issues will differ. If you seek to keep your partner close because of trust issues (say, for instance, your partner cheated on you), then your partner will need to submit to a more transparent life. We'll further discuss this issue in a later chapter addressing affairs.

If you are keeping your partner close because of issues from your own past, you have to find strategies to move beyond that. To help, consider other interests. If you have some existing interests, pursue them. If you don't have any other interests you need to cultivate or develop some.

If you cannot think of an interest beyond your partner, you may have to try different things. You can find options to try by reading course outlines at universities and colleges, by researching activities at local recreational centers and by inquiring at community information centers for possible volunteer activities. There are many places to go where you can be exposed to a variety of things you may find of interest. Even if you try something and find it not to your liking, your exploration already gives some breathing space to your partner and some content for new discussions with each other.

If you have an interest but don't know how to pursue it and worry about how to start, consider taking a class to develop your interest, engaging in volunteer work or applying for an employment situation that includes your interest.

Like to read? Volunteer at a library; join a book club; become an editor. Like gardening? Get a job at a nursery; join a floral society; volunteer at a botanical garden. Like sports? Volunteer as a coach or join a team.

As you pursue your interests, you are out on your own and meet like minded people engaged in the activity of your interest. You develop friendships based on shared interests and activities. As you develop those new friendships, you gain a sense of affiliation. While you may not have felt like a member of any particular group in adolescence, in adulthood you are free to pursue your interests without concern for acceptance by others. You attend an activity pursuing your interest, not people. Finding an affiliation and appreciation of persons participating in the shared interest can come naturally and is a common outcome of doing things with others. The key is to concentrate on your interest and seek to enjoy an activity. No one can give you friends but making friends can be the outcome of what you do with others. Further, as you develop your interest, your competency and skill with regard to that interest will likely develop. That too is rewarding and validating.

If you are a shy person who finds it difficult to manage in the company of others, there are options to help you overcome this challenge, assuming you seek to do so. Social workers and psychologists may help you overcome the fear of getting involved and meeting others. You can learn the skills involved in moving beyond yourself and your usual territory. If this is frightening for you, you must realize that you can always control the pace of change, again assuming you are working toward something and not simply faking it.

FINDING A COUNSELOR

If change is scary for you or if you don't know where to start, begin with counseling. Speak to someone with no investment in the outcome. While family and friends are concerned for your well-being, they will have a vested interest in the outcome by virtue of their connection to you. This is unavoidable and very often undermines the value of their input. Even if reasonable, your partner may be wary of the guidance given by your friends or family, particularly as it concerns the partner.

If you seek guidance from a social worker or psychologist, you can explore what has led to your personality style and what keeps you from engaging with others. You can then come to some understanding of what created your style and change it. Or you might be more comfortable with a social worker or psychologist who is less apt to explore the past that led to your present situation and who instead concentrates upon the changes of behavior necessary to achieve your goals. In addition to, or instead of, seeking the guidance of a social worker or psychologist, you can join a group whose goal is to facilitate greater comfort being in the company of others. One such organization is Toastmasters International, a group designed to help people overcome the fear of public speaking by offering a safe environment in which to practice. At regular meetings in many communities, members of Toastmasters practice their public speaking with like-minded and supportive people. This may offer you a destination and a comfortable setting to learn and develop the skills of being in the company of a group of individuals and speaking aloud.

If you have trouble finding your voice and holding your point of view against someone who presents an opposing argument, then assertiveness training may be for you. Assertiveness training enables individuals to speak their minds better, particularly in the presence of those who may oppose and may seek to impose their will on others. Assertiveness training enables individuals to hold their own so their views may be heard and their needs met.

SELF-DEPENDENCE

When you are no longer dependent upon just your partner to fulfill your needs, you develop not only a range of friendships, but also, in many cases, a sense of purpose that enlivens your perspective on life. Further, you gain the confidence to speak your mind reasonably and improve the likelihood of being heard and meeting your needs.

When you stop blaming your partner for not meeting all your needs and take responsibility for meeting some on your own, you will be a happier, more pleasant and interesting person. Then the time you share with your partner can be appreciated for what you can give to each other and do for each other. You can enter your relationship with a stronger, more independent sense of self, not wholly reliant on any one person to meet all your emotional needs. Further, you will have developed a group of acquaintances and friends who can be a support network for you as life challenges you with trials and tribulations. Indeed, the more friends one has, the more likely one will overcome the many normal challenges that occur. Most men and women face some degree of economic hardship at some point in time as well as job loss or change, illness of self or a loved one and, at some point, the death of a loved one. Having a circle of friends for support at these times of hardship enables better coping and the likelihood of assimilating those experiences into one's life such that one can continue to live and meet the demands of life.

The challenge in this, though, is to stop projecting your upset at the situation onto your partner and to take personal responsibility.

To the degree you can do that, you are then empowering yourself— taking charge of your life to meet your needs. This is a very liberating experience that can actually enhance the quality of your intimate relationship. You will be an emotionally healthier person, not out of dependency and fear, but out of a mutual attraction and common desire based on each other's attributes, not weaknesses.

Molly's Story Continues

Remember Molly? Because she had been so involved with Frank, her circle of girlfriends was small and so her relationship with her new partner, Jim, took on much more significance than might have been the case if she had other friends.

Molly's new boyfriend grew tired of her reliance on him. He tried pulling away as his strategy to force her to be more self-reliant. Molly took this as rejection and sought counseling with the view of bringing him closer. As the therapist explored Molly's background, the therapist came to view Molly as insecure and dependent upon her boyfriend to a great extent. The therapist shared her views with Molly, who reluctantly agreed. Molly was tasked by the therapist to enroll in a class and to develop a hobby. No emphasis was placed on her making new friends.

Fortunately, Molly followed through with the therapeutic advice and took a course in horticulture. She also volunteered at a local botanical garden. Molly's interest in horticulture grew, as did her time in her volunteer activity. As a result, she developed friendships with colleagues and fellow volunteers in pursuit of mutually-satisfying activities. Her attention to her boyfriend diminished and their relationship remained intact and even improved with time. Jim took pride in Molly's accomplishments and attended events with her at her college and at the botanical garden.

NEGLECT

If you are the partner whose attention falls too easily to friends and your attention to others results in discourteous behavior to your intimate partner then you too have some fixing to do. It is one thing to be a good friend and neighbor; it is quite another when your partner feels subordinated and second class in what should be your relationship of priority. Not meeting the needs of your partner, not being available when there is need, believing it is okay that your partner constantly waits on you—these are the hallmark indicators that you are neglecting your intimate partner. These behaviors will distress your relationship. Remember, both men and women may be at fault in these relationship problems.

Sharon's Story

Everyone considered Sharon a good woman. Although she didn't have a paid job, she worked tirelessly as a volunteer at a retirement residence. She always remembered how her mother was so well looked after at the end of her life and felt strongly that she should give back by helping the elderly.

Sharon also felt she never received the adoration or love she needed from her mother, so volunteering with the elderly gained her the appreciation she craved from the residents and also from staff who saw her as keen, lively and very beneficial in terms of enlivening the mood of the residents. As the accolades for her involvement and cheery disposition grew, her attention to home life and the needs of her husband diminished. Her husband, Doug, was a simple guy. He worked long hours at the foundry, helped out with their two young children and did his share of household chores.

However, as time passed, Sharon took her husband more and more for granted. She no longer prepared Doug's lunch in the morning before he left for work and often left him to fend for himself at dinner time. He didn't complain but picked up the extra slack in chores. Yet Doug suffered from Sharon's view that he wasn't caring enough or expressive enough of his feelings for her.

They went to therapy together and Sharon learned that while her husband had to learn to be more expressive of his caring, Sharon had to realize that she was more neglectful of the relationship than Doug and that he felt depressed living under the strain of his increased workload at home and Sharon's increased absence. Doug missed his wife.

Sharon and Doug also came to understand how Sharon, not fully getting her childhood emotional needs met by her mother, was led to seek the attention and validation of others. This was exacerbated by Doug, who needed to learn to be more expressive of his affection, one of Sharon's reasonable needs.

Due to her realizations, Sharon reduced her volunteer hours, concentrating on being more available and supportive of her husband and he, in turn, learned to be more expressive of his affection and appreciation of her.

Max's Story

Max was always a self-absorbed partner. He loved his teenage years and was the type of guy who had many "near misses" in a number of his adolescent adventures. His band of friends had a close bond and he couldn't foresee altering or lessening his social time with the boys.

When Max courted Teri, his current partner, he showered her with flowers, dinners and attention. But a year later he was back to his old ways with his friends and other interests, expecting his partner to be patient with him and tolerate his many late-night returns home and forgotten chores. Teri grew increasingly frustrated. Despite Teri registering her distress with him, Max proceeded with a sense of entitlement, believing that because he felt his ways were okay, that was reason enough to continue.

Teri finally resorted to threats of leaving and made many requests for couples counseling. Max called her bluff and never attended counseling. Finally Teri left Max, realizing she didn't want to be turned into a nagging, despondent housewife. Her staying would have only empowered him. That would have been her contribution to a distressing situation.

DISTANCE AND CLOSENESS

Even if you believe your behavior and view of the situation is acceptable and that issues in the relationship originate with your partner,
being intransigent will not improve your relationship. Intransigence,
a steadfast holding on to doing things your own way, is being stubborn and inflexible. If your behavior and attitude are putting others'
needs before your partner's needs, such as your being late or unavailable for certain events, and if you truly want to maintain the relationship, you have some changing to do. You have to demonstrate that
your partner is the priority. You have to give more *we time* and your
behavior must be courteous and respectful, not just in terms of saying
please and thank you, but by doing what you say you will do when you
are supposed to do it. Good relationships are like an investment. If
you don't make deposits of time and energy and attention into your
investment, it will not grow and may decline.

To improve matters, be home when you say you will be home.
Make time for your partner. Do things together. Have a date night
at least once a week. Attend to household tasks. Tell your partner
directly of your love for him or her.

If you are still unsure about how distant you are from your partner, then count. Count the number of hours you are away at work,
commuting, with friends, with other family, doing your own activities. Then count the number of hours you are with your partner.
Count the number of times in a week you tell your partner you care
about him or her. Count how often you do something with your partner and your partner does something for you. This counting is not
about determining a tit-for-tat arrangement of doing things, but to
set up a more objective determination of whether there is an imbal-
ance of attention. Upon this objective evaluation, make adjustments
to restore the balance and engage in those activities that typically
nurture a relationship, such as doing things for each other, spending
time together and expressing care and love. No garden grows uncultic-
vated, nor does any relationship.

As you engage in behaviors aimed at bringing balance to the relationship, even though you may feel you are losing out in other areas, I hope that the improved satisfaction you derive from the relationship is reason enough to continue, serves as the reward for your efforts and motivates you to persist. As you make these efforts, it is reasonable that your partner should be appreciative and I advise that partner to express his or her appreciation for your efforts.

Partners need to support each other in a relationship and be expressive of their appreciation. This is not sucking up and brown-nosing. Showing appreciation is a kind and loving act that facilitates motivation and creates good feelings between partners.

The Winner's Motto:
I put my partner before my friends and find balance in meeting my needs.

Not Sharing the Chores

The Sinner's Motto:
Clean it yourself.

The quality of relationships is often determined in the small, quieter areas of life. I remember several years after my father died, my mother began seeing a man. He was a very nice man whom she went on to marry. However, my mom was ambivalent about getting too close in the beginning of the relationship. We talked about her feelings and ambivalence. Was it the finances? No. Was it health concerns? No. Was it where you might choose to live? No. Then what was it? I asked.

My mom explained to me that she liked to squeeze the toothpaste tube from the middle and she commented on how many people don't like that. Also she liked the toilet paper to dispense from on top and over the roll, rather than from behind and under. She realized that if she were to live with another man, they would have to get used to each other's ways. She realized that these individual differences, although seemingly trivial, could be real sources of daily frustration. She wound up discussing it with her soon-to-be new husband and they sorted it all out. They have enjoyed a marvelous marriage, now the second marvelous marriage for my mother. It doesn't always go that smoothly.

Jolene and Michael's Story

Michael had always been a bit of a jerk, although he sure knew how to turn on the charm. His charm was disarming and once he hooked you, you found yourself giving in to his demands, subtle as they were. Jolene, while naive, fancied herself a liberated woman. Both were living independently when they met. Their courtship was brief and they started cohabiting within just a few weeks of meeting, with Jolene staying over more and more at Michael's apartment. He had a one-bedroom apartment over a store in the city. It was neat and tidy and suited his single needs.

Although they lived mostly at Michael's place, Jolene kept her apartment. They were both young, just setting out in life. Michael did his best to convince Jolene to continue to stay at his place. He also asked her for favors. The favors were typically innocuous, things he could do himself, but things he asked of Jolene: buy cigarettes, open a beer, make a sandwich, clean the toilet.

The toilet wasn't first on his list of requests but came up a few weeks into the relationship. He let Jolene know that prior to her living with him, he hardly ever needed to clean the toilet and projected the decline in tidiness to her use alone. Jolene was sucked into his nonsense at first, but as the weeks dragged on she grew tired of his self-serving requests, subtle demands and expectations to be served—or as she now saw it, to be waited on.

She tried taking more and more of his requests, thinking it would appease him, but eventually she grew tired of it. She decided to let him know forthrightly of her discontent, hoping it would serve as a wake-up call and restore some balance to the relationship.

CONFRONTING

Confronting doesn't equal fighting. The trick is to inform your partner frankly of your expectations concerning his or her share of the household tasks. Why do you have to clean the toilet too? Because you take your turns at making it dirty. The challenge is not picking up the slack for the other person. You can never buy affection by bending to your partner's demands, thinking you are investing in the relationship with all your good deeds. In fact, you are likely setting yourself up to be taken advantage of even more.

Michael backed off on the demands for a bit. Sometime after that, Michael began pressing Jolene to contribute to the rent even though she still maintained her apartment. Jolene decided that enough was enough and ended the relationship, because Michael wasn't great at taking turns or sharing.

Unfortunately, many people look better when trying to impress a potential mate. However, once settled in a relationship, the attitude becomes *I will only do what I have to do. I will try to get away with as much as possible.*

Sandhu and Sarit's Story

Some relationships seem destined for greatness and then hit snags:

Sandhu was twenty-eight and had a good job in accounting. He lived independently in a condominium, moving there from his parents' home two years previously with money he had saved. He didn't have a cleaning service, but he kept an immaculate home. He took pride in his appearance; his clothes were always fresh and his shirts crisp.

Sarit, twenty-five, had a degree from a business program with a concentration in marketing and was remarkably independent, living on her own for a year. Like Sandhu, she made a good living and seemed like the kind of woman who was able to speak her mind.

Although they both came from traditional backgrounds, Sandhu and Sarit prided themselves at adapting to and adopting Western culture. They were the first generation offspring of East Indian immigrant parents. They wrestled their independence from traditional parental expectations. Just living in their own residences was evidence enough that they were different from their parents and their parents' way of thinking. This already enamored them with each other.

Sarit thought she had found her soul mate in Sandhu: handsome, East Indian, independent, capable of taking care of himself and financially stable. Sandhu thought likewise of Sarit: gorgeous, East Indian, Westernized and financially stable in her own right.

In getting to know each other, both Sandhu and Sarit seemed communicative and wondrously supportive of each other. Given their demanding careers, each ran interference for the other to attack the drudgery of mundane chores and tasks cutting into their time together. They were both remarkably giving. He helped her with tidying and cleaning her apartment. She made snacks when his friends were over watching sports. Sandhu and Sarit were seamless as a couple and seemed to complement each other.

Elders on both sides were aware of the family of the other, so while Sandhu and Sarit dated, everyone was supportive of their relationship. If ever there appeared to be a perfect match, this was it.

Sandhu and Sarit married, recognizing that although they were independent, living together was not an option. There was only so much that their parents could tolerate.

The wedding was a spectacular East Indian extravaganza. Sandhu was bedecked as a prince and Sarit, his princess. Everything flowed: the ceremony, the clothing, the decorations, the food, the entertainment and the honeymoon. The start of this marriage seemed perfect and blessings were bestowed upon this couple.

Sandhu and Sarit entered their marriage thoughtfully. They courted for eighteen months prior to marriage and had the support of both families. Money was not an issue and they agreed that upon marriage they would live in Sandhu's condominium rather than Sarit's rented apartment. Sandhu and Sarit could make good joint decisions. These two looked like they were on a fast track to marital success. Even their respective friends complimented them about their choice in each other. Sarit's friends wondered how to find a man so giving and helpful around the house and Sandhu's friends wondered how to find a woman so into sports or at least accepting of typical male activities.

Less than a year passed before Sandhu and Sarit began slacking off. Whether it was the occasional ribbing he got from his friends that he should wear an apron or the teasing Sarit got from her friends for catering to her hubby's habits, both began to begrudge participating in some of the tasks that each had previously appreciated by the other.

As Sandhu was apt to let his turn at washing the dishes slide, Sarit was at the same time less apt to prepare snacks for game-day get-togethers, let alone be available to join.

At first, Sarit accepted Sandhu's excuses of being tired and not having the time to attend to his chores and so she picked up the extra tasks for him. Sandhu accepted Sarit's excuse of having to take time to help her friends. Slowly he conceded the fact that he would have to get his own snacks together to enjoy game day with his friends.

Just past their first anniversary both were experiencing some animosity, each believing the other wasn't contributing equally. It was as if an unspoken covenant had been broken. They began to distance themselves from each other.

As animosity and anger grew, intimacy diminished. Both were increasingly dissatisfied with the relationship and both were becoming more intransigent, resisting giving in to the other's requests. Bad feelings developed.

One day Sandhu blurted out that he thought Sarit should do all of the cleaning, including the toilet, just as his mother had. She snapped back that she never really did like sports and that his interest there was greater than his interest in her, just as she observed in her father.

Both felt betrayed and deceived. They were also distressed to be confronted with being just like the people from whom they thought they were different: their parents. As Sarit portrayed Sandhu as a sexist, traditional man, this confronted his view of himself as a liberal, Westernized East Indian. As Sandhu portrayed Sarit as a dependent, nagging wife, this confronted her self-image as an independent and assertive woman. Both had extremely defensive reactions to the shadow cast by the other upon them.

Do you see yourself in Sandhu and Sarit? The real issue here is the unspoken expectations partners have for each other. When they are smitten in the early stages of a relationship, they may not see each other clearly for who they are, or they may be somewhat chameleon-like, taking on the characteristics that most ingratiate them to another. This is not malevolently motivated nor a manipulation. When smitten, people seek to make themselves desirable to the objects of their affection. They seek to please in order to be liked in return. With that in mind, they present their better selves and typically with a view to what brings pleasure to intended partners.

Once connected, though, partners reveal themselves and they learn who they are in the context of an intimate relationship, which may be different from who they are when not in a relationship and certainly different during the initial stages of infatuation. In the face of disappointment, frustration or dashed expectations, partners reveal another part of themselves yet again. Perhaps most important, partners reveal how they resolve conflict in the context of an intimate relationship. They may be shocked not just by what is revealed about their partners, but also by what is revealed about themselves if or when their own behavior degenerates. Some common realizations include:

> "I really thought he was the one. He was already living on his own, so for sure he had to wash the dishes. I thought

he would naturally carry on doing it once we were together. He was so unlike any other guy I had ever known."

"She was incredible. How many girls do you know who will watch sports with you and let you invite the guys over and then even make some food? She was amazing."

"As much as I was disturbed by what I saw in my partner, I was equally if not more upset by seeing how I managed myself in the situation. I didn't like what I had become."

EARLY RELATIONSHIP BEHAVIOR

At times when a relationship is developing, partners are on their best behavior and, at other times, tolerant of behaviors they would otherwise find unacceptable. The beginning stages of a relationship skew judgment, actions, what partners take offense to and tolerances. They believe that "what they see is what they get," never thinking that the vision before them could change. They jump in with the belief that their new partners are unlike all others. Even in view of a few annoyances, they delude themselves that those annoyances are minimal when weighed against the marvelous, if not exaggerated, attributes of the new and budding love. The euphoria that comes from a new relationship is intoxicating. As partners are overcome with the wondrous attention, their thoughts, feelings and interests "in sync," they are unsuspecting of what lies ahead.

Whether it takes a week, a month, a year or several years, eventually partners cohabit, married or not, and there's a commitment to be defined as a couple. They are in a shared living space. They are in each other's company almost constantly. Soon comes the gradual recognition that the partners are not exactly what they "advertised" at the beginning of the relationship and that they may be stuck with a partner who is not as functional or multi-dimensional as promoted. It's one thing being on your best behavior while a relationship is developing. It's quite another attempting to sustain that mirage forever.

In cohabitation, you usually have only one model to fall back on: your parents' relationship. While the structure of life typically precludes your parents as role models for living on your own, they are the example of what two people look like when living together. Don't pretend that you are very different from your parents. Even if you want to distance yourself from what you saw in your childhood, do you really know anything else? Do you have any other examples of married life that are more potent than that of your own parents? No wonder most people's marriages mirror their families of origin.

Sandhu and Sarit were great on their own, but together found their behavior mirroring that of their parents and, in particular, what they considered the worst traits of their respective parents. There was comfort in falling back into the old familiar patterns they were exposed to growing up, but they were mortified by what they had become and didn't want to identify with their parents' attitudes, behaviors and marital roles. This is not to say there was anything truly wrong with any of their parents; Sandhu and Sarit just wanted to be different in style.

They were faced with the dilemma of change: knowing full well what they didn't want, not wishing to give up all of the old ways, particularly those that were self-serving, and not knowing how to tackle changing what should really change, all while having no role models.

There doesn't have to be a bad guy here. Even if things degenerate and each casts the other in undesirable terms, Sandhu and Sarit come from respected, albeit traditional, families. These are persons who are remarkably goal directed, educated, financially responsible and law abiding. They have good standing in the community and within their social circles. Even with decent people in the best of circumstances, relationships can still run aground and need rescue.

Swimming upstream against the familiar takes effort. Life is easy when going with the flow. If only Sandhu and Sarit could bear with it and live a life based on their parents' structure, things might be less complicated. When one or both spouses are troubled by the circumstances, it's a little like finding a pebble in your shoe. You are fine for the first few steps, but over time the pebble begins to feel like a stone and grows more intolerable. Eventually you are in pain and even though the path of least resistance seemed best at first, it created the greatest distress. So too in a marriage. As my mother taught me, it is okay to ponder the simple things such as squeezing the toothpaste tube, because these little issues are the pebble in the shoe of marriage. Marital distress creates personal and interpersonal turmoil. Annoyances create distress over time and unchecked marital distress creates mental health problems. Chief among those mental health problems are anxiety and depression. With anxiety and depression come sleep and eating disturbances, irritability and dysfunctional behavior.

COMING TO TERMS

Not only were Sandhu and Sarit coming to terms with their marital discord, but also with the impact on their view of the perfect marriage. Their seemingly perfect marriage fell apart. They suffered a fall from grace that felt shameful and embarrassing, especially in view of family and friends. In their shame and embarrassment, neither spoke to others who might provide the support and guidance necessary to get them back on track. Neither wanted to attend counseling, believing this to be an admission of their marital fall from grace, something neither could accept. Instead, they continued to walk with a pebble in their marital shoe. The more the pain, the less the intimacy. The less the intimacy, the greater the emotional divide. Sarit was depressed, sensing the loss of her marriage, and Sandhu was anxious and frightened for what might happen next.

Sarit's mother noticed her daughter's distress. Although she wanted her daughter to be traditional, Sarit's mother also took secret pride in her daughter's adjustment to Western living. It was as if Sarit's mother lived vicariously through her daughter, who became the woman she longed to be. Sarit's mother

discussed with Sarit the challenge of being in a transitional gen-
eration. She spoke about the challenge of being caught in the
middle of being raised traditionally yet in a Western society,
seeking to enjoy the best of both.

Wanting to be independent of her husband yet at the same
time appreciating being available to meet his needs, Sarit
needed to find balance between distancing herself from the tra-
ditional East Indian ways of her mother yet still embracing her
mother's devotion to husband and family. Sarit soon discovered
that doing for one's partner is not a subservient position, but a
statement of caring. Sarit found a way to assimilate both past
and present.

She shared her insights with Sandhu. They discussed his in-
ternal conflict between traditional roles and tasks and that of
this new generation that saw men less stereotypically. They also
talked about both the positives and negatives of those changes:
Sandhu could be a gentle, nurturing man; they needed to share
the chores, what was seen traditionally as women's work.

Given their discussion and insights, Sandhu and Sarit
quickly stabilized their marriage. Sandhu and Sarit took turns
cleaning the toilet and discussed how other household tasks
could be shared reasonably between them.

What if one's mother is not like Sarit's? How does one go about
correcting the course of a marriage that seems off track, not on the
big issues, but because of the little ones? How do you keep from
degenerating and creating behavior that only contributes to distress?

Every marriage is a shaping process. There's what one partner
brings to it and there's what the other partner brings to it. They each
have their own ways of doing things and thinking about things. They
are both used to certain living patterns that they take for granted.

I remember our recent home renovation of the en-suite bathroom and bedroom. Having lived in our home for twenty years, we

knew it needed a refresher. We knocked out the adjacent walk-in closet to accommodate a shower for two as well as separate vanities. Being a handyman myself, I took on the entire task. Together my wife and I accomplished the renovation and lived to tell the tale. However, what followed was several months of adjustment. I consciously had to think about where to put my toothbrush, my razor and my shampoo. Although the renovation was happily anticipated and invited, what was once an easy morning routine was now a carefully thought-out exercise imposed by the new bathroom. Many mornings both my wife and I were without towels, having forgotten to bring them over for when we exited the shower stall. With time we got used to the new structure and relocation of our toiletries. Our behavioral routines were reshaped.

Marriage is similar. You are accommodating to changes in structure, in this case social structure, where both spouses are living and adapting. In a marriage, just as you are seeking to adjust, so is your partner and, as such, the process may appear awkward. At the same time, the physical structure of your life has changed. Even if you are in the same residence as before, there are accommodations necessary for the items of the other person and that requires some degree of adaptation too.

The process of change or adaptation may be frustrating, particularly when beyond what may have been anticipated. You may have thought that you and your partner were completely compatible. You can recognize that the layout of a home cannot change to suit you, but you may believe that a living entity such as your spouse can adjust to accommodate you. While you may consider yourself flexible, there may be an expectation that your partner concede more on certain issues than yourself. However, the best adaptation in the context of a relationship is achieved when both spouses partake in the process and both make accommodations for each other.

The issue for Sandhu and Sarit was that they didn't talk things through. Perhaps it was the naivety of being young or the thought of having so much in common, but Sandhu and Sarit were blindsided by the degree to which marriage requires adaptation and accommodation. Sandhu and Sarit were held back in receiving help by a sense of shame and embarrassment.

Part of what was keeping a poor situation going was the difficulty both Sandhu and Sarit had dealing with the perceptions of others toward them. In part, ego got in the way of both. Neither was quite able to withstand the embarrassment. They both were waiting for the other to initiate change. Fortunately for them, Sarit's mother helped identify the issue and then this couple was able to make their adjustments.

The first objective in addressing household chores and expectations with your partner is admitting when you are upset or feeling shame or embarrassment so you can get it out of the way. This is known as meta-communicating: communicating about your feelings to set up a dialogue about the issues giving rise to your feelings. The conversation starts like this:

I need to discuss something with you, but I am a little embarrassed about raising this issue. I even feel somewhat shameful that I wasn't able to sort this out by myself. Can I talk with you about it?

This kind of conversation opener is both non-defensive and non-offensive. It sets the stage for the listener, your spouse, to be compassionate, given that you are trying to say something that is difficult for you. After that you can address the real issue of concern: the sharing of household tasks and expectations.

Who cleans the toilet is really part of a larger conversation with regard to mutual expectations around household chores. Very often people enter into relationships assuming that each partner knows what is expected of the other, whether it is who does what or when things get done. Avoiding this discussion can cause bad feelings to fester and cause bigger problems.

Once engaged in the conversation about the household chores, you can readily admit what you like to do, what you don't like to do, how often you feel things should be done, what conditions trigger addressing household tasks and what the criteria for completion is.

Cohabiting takes certain skills and this discussion is one of them. As you are talking with your partner, the key is not to run too fast to fix anything. This tends to be more difficult for men, who sometimes believe they can and must fix everything—and quickly. The key is not to fix a thing but to have a meeting—think business meeting, informational and dispassionate—where you explore the various issues, backgrounds, attitudes and solutions before running headlong to the first or perhaps the most obvious solution. While taking turns may be a simple answer to sorting out household chores, if the criteria for successful completion isn't the same for both partners, you still have a setup for conflict. Take your time to think and talk this through.

While taking turns on any particular task may seem like the best solution, it may just be the worst. What if one of you doesn't have the particular strength or skill for a given task? What if one of you absolutely abhors doing a required household chore? What if a chore is inconvenient for a person?

I happen to hate mowing the lawn, which my wife doesn't mind doing. To split this chore fifty-fifty may sound fair, but would create a condition where I was unhappy in my task and she was missing out on something she enjoys. I love to cook and while my wife is a good cook, it's not her favorite thing to do. So again, divvying this up fifty-fifty also doesn't make complete sense. By talking about these tasks, though, we come to learn about each other's preferences, likes and dislikes. Nowadays she is apt to mow the back lawn, but asks that I cut the front, because the slope there makes it harder for her to push the lawnmower. This is an outcome that respects our different preferences and respects our different physical strengths. As for the cooking, whenever I get the chance, I cook. The demands of my work life interfere with my cooking daily, but I don't hesitate to cook dinner when I can, which is often several times a week, usually on weekends. So rather than divvying tasks up equally, which you can still do, look at preferences and practical considerations such as work schedules, availability and physical ability.

As for practical considerations, think about your daily routines. These are often organized around work hours and, if you have children, school hours and extracurricular activities. You and your spouse may be available at home at different hours. It may be that one partner arrives home first on particular days and the other partner arrives home first on other days. It may make sense for the one arriving first to prepare dinner or manage the children or tackle a certain chore to provide for more couple time when both are available. Alternately, the person arriving home first may appreciate a little time alone to which both may agree and then choose to participate in chores together as a joint activity. It doesn't matter how you choose to divvy up the tasks of joint living as long as you are both in agreement.

Beyond practical considerations, you, your partner or both of you may believe that some tasks are better divvied up based on gender. Some people believe strongly that there are tasks for women and tasks for men. Stereotypically, men are involved in the outside work and maintenance and women in the inside work. Thus women are apt to take responsibility for cooking, cleaning and childcare and men are apt to take responsibility for yard work and home maintenance. If this works for you and your spouse, then so be it. The only caveat is that these decisions should be made jointly. If either of you is dissatisfied with the outcome, then your relationship is at risk for conflict. While you may be able to live with a situation that is less than desirable now, the challenge will be living with it on a daily basis year after year. This is not to say that couples can't renegotiate down the road. In fact, you and your spouse can renegotiate at any time and I encourage this, but facing the issue in the first place is the best way to start.

It may be that what worked in the beginning doesn't work now for any number of reasons. Things change, attitudes change, circumstances change and so can how couples divvy up their tasks. Illness, death of a loved one, change of job or loss of job can be potent disrupters. Getting tired of the routine can also be a potent disrupter. Family life and associated tasks may need to be rearranged too to accommodate these other intervening situations. Divvying up household tasks is not a one-time discussion or activity, but an ongoing process where the plan is always subject to reevaluation based on new or shifting circumstances.

SANDHU AND SARIT MOVE ON

Having opened up the conversation, Sandhu and Sarit were surprised at just how traditionally minded they both were, despite having previously seen themselves as liberal in their thinking. Sarit took pride in preparing Sandhu's meals and in having his friends over on game day with him taking joy in her treats for the guys.

Sandhu came to realize that Sarit felt somewhat demeaned by cleaning the toilets but was okay with doing some of the laundry. With that and given Sarit's contribution to cooking, he readily accepted that he would be responsible for cleaning the toilets.

Now, instead of withholding things from each other, Sandhu and Sarit were apt to discuss matters, having learned that with level heads and non-defensive, non-offensive talk, they were free to discuss and bring issues to resolution. They also learned that although they were more traditional than anticipated, they strove to be less traditional than their parents. They agreed that they would work to move outside their comfort zones and develop broader skill bases to handle a greater range of chores between them.

This was a fantastic outcome for Sarit and Sandhu, because they learned that if one or the other wasn't available to meet a particular need, the other could do it and their lives could proceed with less interruption.

Perhaps you are in a same-sex partnership and worry that how you divvy up the household tasks says something uncomfortable about your roles from a gender perspective. Consider Sandhu and Sarit. Gender may have provided a minor issue, but more potent were issues that gave rise to embarrassment or shame. Once these were overcome, both were able to speak with each other about respective concerns. This holds true for same-sex partners with the overlay of socio-cultural norms at times imposing additional dimensions for discussion.

Marta and Dominique's Story

Marta and Dominique considered each other soul mates. They met each other at a rally for gay rights. Dominique, a woman three years older than Marta, came from a family where her sexual orientation was readily accepted. Dominique never questioned her sexual identity or felt the need to keep it secret from herself or her family; it was simply never an issue.

This was different from Marta. The rally was part of Marta's coming out process: it was her first public appearance as a gay woman. The experience was as frightening as it was liberating. She had left home a few years prior, seeking to keep her sexual orientation hidden from her family, but also wanting to develop a small, private lifestyle in keeping with her real identity. News of her attendance at the rally reached her parents and this precipitated her coming out to her family and the world.

Dominique was proud of Marta and a staunch supporter of her living as her true self. Marta's parents eventually came around to their daughter's new relationship, but neither Marta nor Dominique ever felt their relationship and sexual orientations were truly accepted by Marta's parents, even though Marta's parents were polite about it.

When it came to making decisions about who did what, Dominique was pretty much at ease with anything. Marta needed much time to consider and weigh the meaning of each determination. She carefully considered any decisions with a view to gender stereotypes and concern that Dominique may have her cast in a particular role with regard to their relationship.

One day Dominique called Marta and asked her to clean the toilet. That evening, seeing looks of consternation on Marta's face, Dominique recognized Marta's internal struggle. Without taking offense, she guessed that Marta was weighing her views on the matter of household expectations against gender stereotypes.

Dominique opened up a dialogue with Marta. She began by saying she thought Marta was ill at ease about something and wondered what was on her mind. This left an opening for Marta and she gingerly told Dominique that she had trouble figuring out the basis of some of Dominique's views on the sharing of household tasks. Marta really wondered why Dominique had called to have her clean the toilet.

Dominique asked Marta if she thought that Dominique was trying to cast her in some specific role within their relationship. Marta was both taken aback and pleased by Dominique's insight and she answered yes. This led to a productive discussion about gender issues within same-sex relationships and the roles that partners may be perceived as taking on or having imposed upon them.

Dominique told Marta that she had asked Marta to clean the toilet because it needed cleaning and Marta was arriving home first before their dinner guests were due to arrive. Dominique explained she didn't want Marta to be embarrassed if their friends used the bathroom, given how dirty it was.

With that, Marta realized she was carrying too much emotional baggage as she adjusted to coming out and to her relationship with Dominique as a gay woman.

Part of marital life is in the small details of everyday living. Toilets get dirty and toilets need cleaning. Along the way we imbue this and other simple tasks with all sorts of meaning. These issues need to be discussed and resolved.

Now is the time to sit down with your partner to engage in the type of conversation that can lead to resolution. First, meta-communicate:

"I have something to discuss with you that I feel awkward raising." Second, raise the issue: "Our approach to dealing with the household chores isn't working for me. I was hoping we could discuss it and come to a resolution." Third, be more specific: "I think we have different standards of clean and I would like to figure out who should be responsible for what and when."

Now, you could skip right to a resolution or instead move toward learning more about yourselves: How did your parents manage these issues when you were growing up? The challenge in this type of discussion is staying with the learning versus marching directly to the resolution. The benefit of continuing the learning is that when a resolution is finally achieved, there is a greater likelihood that it is more reflective of who you both are as persons so that there will be better follow-through on what was resolved.

> "I feel like a wuss when I clean. I was always taught to
> think that cleaning was women's work."

> "I actually think it's sexy when you clean. When you clean,
> I see you as more of a man."

(Note to men: There is some research to suggest that women find men who do housework more attractive. From the women's perspective, they perceive these men as loving and caring. Women are more likely to get in the mood for intimacy if their partners take on the chores.)

Resolutions are only as good as they are kept. Think of all the New Year's resolutions that people make, most often to lose weight. Statistically, only 12 percent actually keep their New Year's resolutions according to Richard Wiseman of the University of Hertfordshire in *The Guardian's* article "New year resolution? Don't wait until New Year's Eve." That's a low success rate and you don't want your resolution to fall into that category. That is why the process—the discussion in advance of your resolution—is so important. You want to understand the variables that may intervene to throw your resolution off track so you can plan to manage those if and when they arise.

Discussion is everything. In the end, who cleans the toilet is less important than how it gets decided, and how it gets decided should be a mutual decision.

The Winner's Motto:
I clean what I help make dirty and appreciate that chores are meant to be shared.

Thinking It's Your Money

The Sinner's Motto:
If I earned it, I can spend it.

Wrapping one's mind around the concept of money—who makes it, who owns it, who gets to use it and for what—is a challenge in many relationships. It is common that one partner has short-term goals and sometimes very short-sighted goals while the other partner has long-term goals, sometimes so long term there is never any pleasure in the present. The fight may be big-screen television set versus bigger house with a baby's room or new car versus retirement planning. The challenge is to gain perspective and plan so that both views are accommodated. You may have to consider learning to manage debt and you have to come to terms with whose money it is anyway, despite who earns what. As you continue to read this chapter, remember that as with any example provided, the genders can easily be reversed or be the same in a couple. You have to ask yourself, *Do I see myself in any of the examples and, if so, what does that mean for me in terms of what I may have to do differently?*

Millie and Charlie's Story

Millie and Charlie were only married five months when the bills started rolling in.

Shoes, handbags, boots, tableware, sheets, lighting, wall hangings, curtains, cosmetics, electronics, toiletries and clothing were just some of Millie's purchases. Millie's shopping was so extensive that she even devised a way to keep much of it hidden from Charlie. Some purchases she made in cash and others with credit. Some were a combination of cash and credit to make it seem like the cost was less than it actually was. Still other items were purchased on her sister's credit with the promise of repayment. Millie's closet was so full of clothes that when she brought home something new, she quickly and quietly removed the store tag to hide the item right in the closet.

Meanwhile, Charlie was trying to make ends meet. Even though they both worked and earned well, there was never quite enough money to cover the bills. On a month-to-month basis, they were getting deeper and deeper in debt.

Charlie tried discussing their finances with Millie, but she played dumb. She refused to believe they could be in as bad a shape as Charlie said. She whined to Charlie about what she needed next. Charlie caved in and paid the bills.

As their debt grew, Charlie, who was stressed and nervous, began taking antacids. Millie was oblivious, happy and very much indulged. Then Charlie began having anxiety attacks. When they occurred, he looked pale, sweated and had trouble breathing. He kept all this to himself.

Then came the day a really high bill arrived. Charlie had a panic attack. Beyond the usual symptoms, his chest ached and his heart pounded. He felt like he was dying. Being at home he was unable to hide it from Millie, who thought he was having a heart attack and called 911. Charlie was taken by ambulance to the hospital. After an EKG, his heart was deemed normal as was his blood work. He was prescribed a medication for anxiety and told to cut down on the antacids given concerns of side effects with excessive use. It was suggested that he and Millie see a marital therapist to address the source of his anxiety.

Charlie entered therapy with a sense of relief. Now Millie was the one experiencing anxiety.

One of the areas the therapist explored was their respective knowledge of household finances, such as home insurance, car insurance, mortgage, utilities and bank accounts. Millie had no knowledge on all these concerns. Charlie knew each answer exactly.

Then it came time for true confessions. Millie disclosed her spending habits and secret purchasing methods and hiding places. Charlie felt deceived. Millie was disgraced. Then the therapist gave them homework.

Charlie was to make a spreadsheet listing all their expenses against income. He was to account for their expenses for the past thirty days relative to their joint income. Where he couldn't account for debt, that was the shortfall, likely attributable to Millie's secret spending.

Charlie and Millie returned to the therapist the following week. Charlie presented his spreadsheet. Charlie and Millie were falling into debt at the rate of $2,500 monthly with a five-month accumulated debt load of $12,500 in consumer debt. Charlie also explained to Millie that he increasingly couldn't sleep and couldn't foresee affording the mortgage payment in the near future.

Through therapy Millie began to realize that her behavior was deceitful, not a flattering self-evaluation. She also began to realize that in taking advantage of the man she loved she was undermining their financial security, their life together and Charlie's health. Sheepish to start, she began to take the program seriously.

Millie absolutely had to reduce her spending. Indeed, there would be no discretionary spending until after the debt was retired. Also, the couple had to achieve some understanding of how and for what they wanted to save. Would they be saving for the cost of having and raising children? Children's education? Retirement? Replacement vehicles? Vacations?

It is hard to appreciate where your money goes if you don't track it. Millie gave up her credit card and she was allowed strictly cash purchases and only for essentials. Charlie withdrew money from the bank on a weekly basis for Millie and for every penny spent, Millie and Charlie had to account for their outlays with receipts.

Millie had to list her purchases in a ledger and organize them into categories of her choosing. She saw that the items on her list almost naturally fell into certain categories, such as toiletries, household supplies and food. This showed Millie where her money was being spent on a day-to-day basis with normal purchases for everyday living. Millie then had to compare those expenditures with income and learn about the other costs they had as a couple: mortgage, vehicle maintenance, utilities and school loans. This series of exercises served as a wake-up call as Millie now had tangible evidence of what it cost to manage their household. To rescue their marriage, both Millie and Charlie had to be committed to a drastic change in behavior, new learning and goal setting.

Even though Millie took therapy seriously and worked on her problem, retiring $12,500 in consumer debt didn't come easy nor did deciding how to rein in spending and set financial priorities.

Charlie and Millie added the debt to their mortgage to reduce the interest, but they still had to lower their monthly budget by $2,500 in overspending in order to account for debt (mortgage) repayment as well as to have money to set aside for saving toward other financial objectives. Together they earned in excess of $100,000 and given the size of their mortgage (nice house, nice location), the payments on their vehicles (SUV and sports car), something else had to give. They really had to account for an additional $4,000 a month—$48,000 per year—either with additional revenue or cost control.

It can be unimaginable to consider downsizing one's home, driving a less desirable vehicle or giving up a vehicle entirely, hunting for better-paying employment or taking on a second and sometimes even a third job. Not only did Millie have to give up spending on herself, but something else had to be chopped.

Millie and Charlie decided to give up their trendy downtown townhome to relocate just outside of the city. They not only managed to reduce their mortgage payments, but also wound up with a larger detached home. Both their vehicles were traded in for one that was more economical and they found a way to shuttle each other to the train station to commute to work. Not only were they meeting their financial objectives but also they found money in the budget to travel on vacation. They reviewed their lifestyle, discussed health issues and family planning. They took on the kinds of discussions and made the kinds of decisions that rekindled their spark and their relationship. Finances improved and children followed.

While their parents were proud, their friends were befuddled. Their friends couldn't believe Charlie and Millie's decision. The friends, not mean spirited, but not appreciating the scope of the problem, kept extolling the virtue of a lavish lifestyle and kept reminding Charlie and Millie what they were giving up. They kept focusing this couple on their losses: loss of status, loss of possessions, loss of indulgences.

Even though a great outcome, the path to solvency was not a straight line and was fraught with upsets and tension. Millie and Charlie had to come to terms with their change in lifestyle and the loss of their unsustainable fantasy, particularly in view of their friends' not-so-subtle reminders. In the face of it all, they had to develop a mantra to help them through the changes, to help them overcome their friends seeking to maintain the status quo.

On a moment-to-moment basis, Charlie and Millie reminded themselves by placing a message on their refrigerator door: "Our marriage and well-being is worth more than the trappings of an unsustainable lifestyle."

In Borneo, a southeast Asian island, monkey teeth are a possession prized by the natives as a sign of prosperity. The challenge, though, is in acquiring the monkeys' teeth. For that, native hunters craft a trap that ingeniously captures the monkey. They take a gourd, a hard-skinned vegetable, cut a small hole in the middle and remove the fleshy interior through the hole. They then place a small piece of fruit into the gourd and, using reeds, latch the gourd to a branch in a tree to entice a monkey.

A monkey seeking to obtain the fruit narrows its hand to squeeze through the hole in the gourd. With its hand in the gourd, it is then free to grab the fruit. However, with its hand now clenched in a fist around the fruit within the gourd, it is too big to withdraw and the monkey's hand is stuck inside the gourd. The monkey, not willing to let go of its prize, remains snared with its hand in the gourd. It's trapped. Along comes the hunter with a machete. The hunter lops off the monkey's head and gains the prize: the monkey's teeth. The teeth are woven into a bracelet—a monkey tooth bracelet. I have one such bracelet, given to me by my brother from a trip to the Far East. It serves me as a potent reminder of the moral of the story: If you don't want to lose your head, let go of the prize.

Millie and Charlie learned this lesson well. Millie let go of the entrapment of all her purchases and the acquisition of material goods. She let go of the obsession of concerning herself with how well off she looked in the eyes of her friends from a material perspective. She let go of believing she could have anything she wanted and could enjoy a lifestyle beyond her means. As for their friends, some eventually understood it and some didn't. To those who did, Millie and Charlie were role models of how to achieve financial stability in married life.

Not everyone makes that kind of recovery from the brink. Some couples may learn to keep themselves from going over, but unfortunately they continue to live life on the edge. Barry and Julia were one such couple.

Barry and Julia's Story

Barry and Julia went to therapy to address Barry's spending. Barry sought to indulge himself and his family with everything. To him, money was no object. Barry was completely open about his spending. Barry's spending and openness about his purchases frustrated Julia.

A lot of his shopping was for their children and the family. He felt that his children should have everything, that his family should be able to enjoy life and so should he. Barry had his own mantras that he repeated any time Julia challenged him. If purchasing for himself, "I deserve it" and if for the family, "We deserve it." Soon this deserving family found themselves facing mortgage foreclosure.

Barry came not only from a family of limited means, but also from a family where his parents took little interest in him. Indeed, his parents treated him as if he was an object for their use. "Get me a beer" was a common refrain from a dad who was unavailable to go to his son's baseball games. His mom requested Barry run errands and then admonished Barry, saying his return was never as swift as expected. Praise and affection were nonexistent.

Barry never felt valued. He did well at school in the hopes this would gain his parents' admiration. Nothing. He got a good job thinking that would gain their admiration. Nothing. He was attentive to his parents' needs and demands, even in adulthood and in spite of the turmoil this created in his marriage. Julia could never understand how Barry so continually gave to his parents when nothing was reciprocated. Barry just kept defending his parents, saying they deserved it, as did he and his family when he overextended himself financially.

Barry was chasing the dream of one day feeling valued by his parents. His incessant spending was also about him compensating for his own limited self-worth, replacing what he didn't get from his parents, trying to prove to himself that he was of value and did deserve something. Barry was trying to fill an emotional hole and yet doing so was undermining his marriage and his family's financial well-being. Barry was very much an emotional spender.

It was a tough lesson for Barry to learn that his parents would never be forthcoming with the kind of adoration of which he was deprived in childhood. Letting go of chasing the fantasy of receiving his parents' love and respect caused him to feel like an abject failure and worthless as a person. Even though he continued to pursue those ideals from his parents, they would never come and, in the pursuit, Barry inadvertently reconfirmed his feeling that he was of little value. The situation was one of emotional neglect creating a form of emotional abuse. As Barry continued in his pattern of seeking parental validation, he also participated in creating the conditions for his continued abuse.

At some point in life we all separate from our families of origin. We set out into the world to become our own persons. We have gained a good sense of self from the care, love and validation provided by our parents, creating a belief that we are of value and able to attain our dreams. In cases of emotional neglect, some people can never quite disconnect from those who were neglectful. As odd as this seems, it is because within the adult is the child who seeks the parental goodies, enabling it to move on with the adult task of independence. This would-be adult is still a child inside with an unrealized belief that if separated from the parents, the child would lose the opportunity, albeit a false opportunity, of gaining a sense of wholeness and personal value.

Barry's spending was his way of trying to prove to himself and others that he was of value. Every time he said, "We deserve it," he was looking for validation from his family. When he said, "I deserve it," he was trying to convince himself he was deserving.

The challenge in helping people like Barry is in supporting them to stop chasing the dream of parental validation in lieu of forming a more realistic appraisal of their parents' shortcomings, so the pursuit can end. Barry had to come to appreciate that he was of value, independent of his parents' praise, attention or validation. If Barry was able to resist running to meet his parents' demands and withstand their clear and self-serving disapproval, then he stood a chance to separate, form a boundary and take charge of his own sense of self, well-being and validation. Paradoxically, when he met his parents' demands, seeking approval, he was subject to more disappointment. If he were to relinquish his pursuit, he would validate his own self-worth and, in the end, feel better about himself. This change requires a remarkable leap of faith and is even more difficult in the face of a partner who also may be critical.

The challenge for the partner of the likes of a Barry is to be a cheerleader of efforts toward independence—stretching and breaking his nagging fear that as he separates, so too does the perceived source of emotional sustenance. It is too often unrecognized by one's partner that this thrust toward independence takes remarkable courage and faith. A supportive partner can go a long way toward bridging the sense of loss until the benefits of independence begin to take hold.

Julia wanted Barry to be independent from his parents and, more so, wanted him to stop the spending that was putting their home at risk. She appeared to understand that Barry needed support, but in view of the real threat of losing their home, she had no patience or tolerance. From her perspective, the psychological reasoning was interesting but would have to result in an immediate change.

Julia couldn't tolerate delay and cheerleading a grown man seemed ridiculous to her. The challenge in therapy was finding a strategy to manage the financial crisis while at the same time facilitating Barry's emotional separation from his parents, all balanced against Julia's reasonable, yet all-consuming fears.

In situations such as Barry and Julia's it is important to bring in allied professionals to address matters that are more than just relational. In this situation, this couple needed good guidance from a financial professional to address their debt problem. The financial professional also acted as a liaison between the couple and their mortgage holder, negotiating a solution to keep them from insolvency. Within the therapeutic and relationship context, Barry had to learn to consult with Julia prior to any spending and realize that her views and concerns were reasonable. To do so, Barry had to let go of his mantra that they deserved it.

Spending frivolously has nothing to do with being deserving. Spending frivolously has to do with having a discretionary fund of money and an agreement with your partner as to how much either may spend without the knowledge or consent of the other. No one has the right to buy anything for which they don't have the money. To spend in the absence of an agreement as to how money may be used and to spend beyond one's means is irresponsible.

In this case, Barry's spending had nothing to do with being deserving; he was inadvertently using spending as a means to address his otherwise limited stock of self-worth, trying to prove he was of value to the degree he could lavish money on others and himself. Barry's spending was a reflection of not having his emotional needs met by his parents during his childhood and was exacerbated by his ongoing attempts to win their approval. To make gains in terms of his self-worth and his relationship with Julia, he had to separate emotionally from his parents and he required Julia's support to do so.

Julia and Barry continued to struggle for years. The anger that Julia harbored against Barry's parents for their self-serving behavior and the anger she harbored against Barry for his irresponsible spending got in the way of her ability to direct herself more toward Barry's need for spousal support.

Barry's gains were marginal. He managed to have less of a reaction to the pulls of his parents and he managed to rein in his spending enough to keep the creditors away. This in turn reduced Julia's anger but not to the point where she could be fully emotionally supportive and provide positive comments to Barry about his changes.

They lived paycheck to paycheck, which was better than accumulating debt, but come time for college, there was no money to send their children for higher education. Barry deluded himself that this didn't matter, but the truth of the situation was that his issues and Julia's resentment kept their children from receiving educations that may have enabled better lives for them. Their vision and ability to take responsibility was shortsighted although enough to survive. Hopefully their children eventually would do more than just survive.

CHILDREN AND EMOTIONAL GROWTH

As children grow, they go through several developmental stages. The preschool years are a particularly rapid period of growth and development when children have to learn to get along with others, share and make nice. As toddlers, children aren't yet ready for these tasks, so their play is more individual and their attention more egocentric. They have yet to develop an appreciation of the needs of others and they are just coming to understand that when they let go of a toy, it will likely be returned later. This is a particularly difficult concept for toddlers to grasp and they usually don't fully until ages three to four. Given toddlers' development, they engage in what is referred to as parallel play. They play alongside others, but not really with others. In order for toddlers to get along, they each must have a ball. As long as each child has his or her own toy, there is peace within the group. These children hold onto their toys saying, "Mine." This is normal; this is expected.

Children enter the next developmental stage, cooperative play, when they are able to get along with others, recognize others' needs separate from their own and realize that a treasured object when released to a playmate will not disappear but will be returned. Rolling a ball back and forth requires cooperation. Cooperation requires a sense of the life of others and trust that when an object of desire leaves, it will return. As children continue to grow and develop, they eventually learn these skills. You can't push a child to cooperate at play before he or she is developmentally ready and has mastered parallel play.

At this stage children play nicely in the sandbox together, share their toys and even begin to concern themselves with the feelings of their playmates. They can recognize when a playmate is upset and that when they give a toy to that child, the child becomes happy. Being less egocentric, children in this developmental stage can take some pleasure in making other children feel better. At the developmental stage of cooperative play, children have a better appreciation of the impact of their behavior upon other children and, with guidance, learn that pleasing or meeting the needs of other children is rewarding. With time and practice, these skills and positive feelings are internalized. They become part of children's experiences, their views of the world and themselves. These skills become part of who they are as people. This is also normal and expected.

These young children grow up and take the skills learned in early childhood into adulthood. A child's ability to share, recognize and meet the needs of others flows through the years and is reproduced in adult relationships. Watch how an adult is able to share with his or her partner and you are gaining a glimpse into that person's early childhood. Not all adults share nicely.

Sandra and Jacob's Story

Sandra saw Jacob as a diamond in the rough; she loved Jacob for the man he could become. Sandra had to tolerate some selfish behavior, because Jacob wasn't good at sharing. He didn't want to give Sandra a taste of his meal when dining, he was adamant that costs be shared equally, he had to have his side of the closet to himself, even though it was partially empty and Sandra's side was overflowing. When it came to money, his was his and hers was hers.

Sandra and Jacob had separate bank accounts and both paid into a third account to share common expenses such as rent, utilities and vacations. If Jacob didn't like Sandra's ideas for vacations then he wouldn't contribute money to the account. Sandra felt powerless, so she always acquiesced on her vacation preferences to accommodate him. Jacob wasn't good at taking turns. He couldn't imagine having his choice for one vacation and Sandra's choice for another.

Sandra knew that Jacob had a rough upbringing, no fault of his own. His mother passed away shortly after his birth. His father worked two jobs and Jacob's care fell to one then another grandparent. His grandparents were well-intentioned people who doted on Jacob, feeling bad about his poor start in life. Jacob was spoiled, indulged and never really had to share, let alone take turns. Knowing his difficult roots, Sandra wanted to take her diamond in the rough and recreate him—give him an attitude makeover.

Sandra saw this as more than her role; this was her job as his partner. After all, Jacob wasn't a bad man. He did no harm to anybody. He was a quiet soul who kept mostly to himself and who was used to living life on his own terms, doing as he wanted when he wanted. This was his normal. Sharing wasn't part of the equation but neither was acting in directly harmful ways. Jacob had neither a bad word nor a good word for anybody. He just led his life quietly, taking care of his own needs and wants.

Sandra begged, cajoled, teased, informed, coerced and nagged Jacob in her attempts to get him to appreciate the needs and wants of others. She desperately wanted him to become a well-rounded man who could take the feelings of others into account when making decisions. She believed he was a good man who could make this leap and become the kind of partner she envisioned. Again, Jacob wasn't a bad man, just a man who couldn't extend himself to take into account others' needs. He just went quietly in one direction: his.

Given his shortcomings, Jacob was a source of frustration for Sandra. There were things in life she wanted that differed from Jacob's wants and as time drew on, it became increasingly clear to her that her needs and wants wouldn't be met over Jacob's. Jacob walked a single path and no matter how hard she tried to get him to see another way, he was stuck in his rut. He just didn't move in a different direction or spend money on something not to his personal liking. "If it's mine and I earned it, then I get to spend it how I want," he always said. There wasn't room for discussion.

Sandra thought that counseling might help Jacob come to understand the impact of his early years upon his ability to share as an adult and be a bit more free when it came to his money and doing things that others might like to do. Jacob obliged Sandra with little fuss, as long as she agreed to pay for the counseling. Sandra was elated at the thought of entering into counseling with Jacob and finally getting him to see the error of his ways to become the man she knew he could be.

In his therapeutic sessions, Jacob was well able to state his views on sharing and money. He said the same things he told Sandra many times before: "If it's mine and I earned it, then I get to spend it how I want." It didn't take the therapist long to figure out that Jacob had no motivation to change and only attended the counseling sessions in an effort to stop Sandra's nagging. The therapist's suggestions that Jacob might make some changes in himself fell flat.

Given this was couples therapy, the counselor addressed Sandra too. What was it about her that she was so invested in Jacob as her project? Sandra was so focused on Jacob's shortcomings that she had no insight into what was driving her in the relationship.

It turned out that Sandra had her own challenging past with an alcoholic father. Sandra was the caretaker of her father, cleaning up after him, putting her father's needs ahead of her own, just as she witnessed her mother doing before her. And just like her mother, she extolled the same point of view that with time and patience, he would change; underneath he was a good man. Sandra was chasing her dream of making something out of Jacob the way she hadn't been able to with her father.

The counselor redirected therapy to focus on Sandra's need to change Jacob, a change that very likely would not be forthcoming. Pursuing a man who, in the end, couldn't meet her needs was Sandra's contribution to the very distress from which she sought relief. This was a crushing insight for Sandra, one she had difficulty accepting. Sandra had three choices: accept that Jacob wouldn't change and learn to live with that fact; stop her pursuit and, if unsatisfied with the relationship, move on; or look for another counselor who would provide her preferred outcome.

Jacob's obvious shortcomings were Sandra's preferred focus. She felt determined to find the key to unlock this man, not realizing she had to unlock herself from the pursuit of unlikely dreams. Life carried on for Sandra and Jacob, counselor after counselor—with her paying the way.

Solutions to Sandra and Jacob's dilemma with money depend on whether Jacob can learn to share, to take turns, and that spending on one's partner can come back in terms of a more satisfying relationship. If so, they both could enjoy a happier life together. But they stuck it out with each other and carried on in their miserable ways. Jacob couldn't seem to learn to share and Sandra couldn't seem to learn she was chasing a dream.

Apart from whose money it is and who gets to spend it, setting financial priorities is another big source of conflict for many couples.

Melanie and Steve's Story

Both Melanie and Steve were excellent handling money. Both earned and both saved. However, they were keenly motivated by different goals.

Melanie believed she shouldn't bother saving for a future not yet determined. She was more inclined to save toward immediate expenditures like furniture, cars and vacations. She didn't overspend or go into debt; she just couldn't see saving for a future beyond the immediate horizon. If you can't see it, why save for it?

Although still young, Melanie's husband, Steve, foresaw a life in retirement, hoping to have enough money to manage well. He longed for the day when he wouldn't have to work and preferred to tuck all his extra money into his retirement savings plan. For Steve, every penny spent today pushed his retirement plans further into the future. He would happily do without another piece of furniture if it meant retiring that much sooner. Steve also concerned himself with having money in reserve for unanticipated expenses.

Melanie's goals were short term and Steve's long term. Neither Steve nor Melanie was vindictive or deceitful. Both were open about and fully aware of their differences and discontent with the views of the other. Melanie saw Steve as a fuddy-duddy who couldn't have fun and couldn't enjoy life in the present. Steve saw Melanie as a spendthrift who would likely be either destitute in old age or unable to enjoy herself later in life, not having sufficient financial resources.

Melanie and Steve fought incessantly about their approaches to saving. Theirs was an either/or battle where neither Steve nor Melanie could relinquish anything to appease the other. Money did go toward new furniture and money did go toward retirement saving, but each spouse cringed at the priority of the other. This made their marriage uncomfortable when new items were brought home or when Steve made his annual contribution to his savings plan. Steve and Melanie could be nasty to each other, particularly in the company of friends, as each tried to demean the other for his or her financial priorities. Things became critical when, at a party, mutual friends asked them to stop their bickering, because it was overshadowing the fun. Their differences finally spilled into public view and both looked maladjusted.

Their marriage was dysfunctional and they agreed that counseling would be a reasonable expense. In Melanie's mind, counseling would bring about a loosening of Steve's purse strings, so he could enjoy himself in the present. In Steve's mind, counseling would facilitate Melanie's appreciation for saving for retirement or for unanticipated expenses. Both were actually motivated by the interests of the other as well as their own. As a free spirit, Melanie thought it would do Steve some good to loosen up; as a saver, Steve thought it would do Melanie some good to have money in reserve in case of unforeseen circumstances.

In the therapist's office, Steve and Melanie quickly opened up. Steve knew that Melanie's father had died at a young age, but Steve didn't realize the impact it had on Melanie in terms of living for the moment. As her dad approached his death, he bemoaned to Melanie how he didn't have enough fun in life and wished that he had spent more along the way to enjoy himself. He knew he couldn't take it all with him, that his wife was still well looked after financially, but he had regrets for not having fulfilled some of the things he would have liked to have done. He felt a loss for vacations never realized, for purchases never made, for renovations never enjoyed. This left a powerful impression on Melanie who, in her mind, was honoring the memory of her father by living a life that he regretted missing.

Steve's experience in life was different. His parents retired early. Because of their early retirement and then changes in the economy, Steve's parents didn't have enough to live on and so had to return to work. Being older, both his parents had to take on jobs of lower status than they had when younger. Unfortunately, no one would hire them in their prior fields. Both parents had enough presence of mind to know they had to work and were responsible enough to do so, but in Steve's mind, he never wanted to be in that situation. So Steve also had a powerful life experience driving his point of view.

Both Melanie and Steve came from loving, caring families, but their life experiences were very different and those life experiences caused them to have different attitudes toward money, saving and financial priority setting. The challenge in therapy was to devise a plan where the needs of both could be reasonably met. For that the therapist referred the couple to a financial planner, in this case to someone regarded as a financial divorce specialist trained in collaborative approaches to settling financial disputes between separating couples.

Financial divorce specialists are individuals trained in financial planning but with a view to helping couples manage competing priorities. They are used to some degree of conflict that could otherwise interfere with the planning process. They are adept at developing multiple solutions based on competing interests, ones where both partners are compelled to see the success of the other as being in their mutual interest. Although not seeking to divorce, Steve and Melanie's constellation of competing needs and interests made consulting a financial divorce specialist a good choice for facilitating a financial plan they could both accept.

Melanie and Steve's first meeting with the financial divorce specialist was to provide and discuss financial information, income statements and expense sheets. Within the first meeting the specialist also got to know them by asking what brought them to consult with a financial planner and what they hoped to achieve. Having already attended couples therapy, they were both able to explain how their respective pasts played out in their present conflict.

The second meeting with the specialist was to review projections based upon Steve and Melanie's individually-preferred strategies for setting financial priorities. This meeting, based on reviewing respective plans with tangible data, revealed much to the couple. Graphs presented by the specialist showed Melanie how her plan would leave them financially short as a couple, particularly in their mid-sixties when they would like to contemplate retiring. The graphic projection demonstrated to her that based on her spending/saving plan, they would likely have to work the entirety of their lives to have the income needed to live.

The graphs based on Steve's projection left them with a far greater retirement income than necessary, given the lifestyle both sought in retirement. To achieve the lifestyle based on what Steve thought he needed to save, they would need to live an austere life along the way, giving up much in terms of enjoyment. It was quite a wake-up call for both and led to an agreement for a third meeting.

At the third meeting, given the goals Steve and Melanie had individually and jointly, the specialist provided some financial projections based on a few different savings models. Steve and Melanie were able to review information on which to base their decisions for spending and saving. They finally came to an agreement on what to save and how much they could spend.

They were also able to acknowledge each other's past as it determined current priorities. With that they were better able to be supportive of each other. Given the input and education provided by the financial divorce specialist and the style in which it was provided, Steve and Melanie not only learned to manage finances better, but also to discuss matters between themselves more reasonably. The situation of demeaning each other in the company of their friends never arose again.

MONEY AND MARITAL DISTRESS

There's a reason why money ranks as the number one issue associated with marital distress and divorce. Money crystallizes people's differences. Money brings out the best and worst of people's pasts. Partners' views on money, who makes it, who spends it, how it is spent and how much is saved, speak volumes about how they were raised and how they view the world. It is at once a private matter and an issue for joint consideration. Spouses take their pasts for granted, as well as their associations to money, saving and spending. They assume their partners have similar views and that their approaches to managing money will be the same. People imbue money with all sorts of meaning and power. For some it is a means to an end and for others the acquisition of money is an end unto itself. Addressing money matters is inevitable in any relationship. The need to survive, the desire for pleasure, issues of status, power and control, righting historic wrongs and satiating unmet needs all play into conflicts over money.

Solving financial conflicts is more than assigning blame. It requires couples to dig deeper to understand what creates their relationship to the meaning of money. They must answer the questions: What does money represent? What does money mean to me?

Only by exploring the answers to those questions can a couple come to understand the issues underlying their money-related conflicts. It's not the money itself. Money is nothing more than an object except when people project their issues onto it and their issues conflict with those of their partners. Coming to agreements on an approach to money as a couple without digging deeper runs the risk of superficial and fragile arrangements that could easily come undone.

Couples must explore their beliefs about money. They must ask themselves what money represents and talk about how those beliefs and representations came about. Couples can explore their differences and, it is hoped, come to the appreciation that a difference is not necessarily a statement on what is right or wrong, better or worse. Assuming a desire to continue as a couple and an interest in accommodating each other's needs and interests, spouses can then search for solutions that account for each person's unique experiences while creating the best conditions for each partner at no particular loss to the other. This takes patience, imagination and outside resources, including therapists, financial specialists, accountants and, at times, friends and family who can separate their interests from those of the couple. For many this is a struggle, but it can be quite successful, as the couples whose money problems we've examined have shown; other times it is not successful at all.

Money sometimes brings a marriage to a complete halt. It's time to come to terms with what drives your relationship with money and discuss these feelings with your partner before your relationship is ruined because of conflicting financial issues.

The Winner's Motto:
Our relationship is richer
when we share and plan together.

Stepping Out on Your Partner

The Sinner's Motto:
We are only friends; we never had sex.

It's only social media, but as you are socializing with your online friend, where does that leave your partner? What if your online friendship moves from words to images? What if this private relationship is offline and out of line or online yet out of sight? When does a friendship become an affair?

Intimacy is a function of sharing important, emotional and otherwise private information between partners. If you share with another person, what's left for your spouse?

Consider this scenario: Your primary intimate relationship, for whatever reason, is unfulfilling. With or without intention, you confide in someone else, perhaps on the Internet, about your marital distress. You find the person you are talking with to be a good listener and this is appealing. With time, you come to the opinion that it is easier to talk with this other person than your primary intimate partner. This creates an affinity, a natural liking for this person. You come to learn or believe that the affinity is mutual and soon an attraction develops. You feel drawn to each other.

This attraction overshadows your current attraction to your partner or spouse. You meet in person. With whatever you tell yourself or hide from yourself, you let yourself be drawn into a relationship that turns physical. Perhaps first a kiss or just a touch. Maybe you are torn between your vow of fidelity and the passion of the moment. You teeter on the edge and find yourself falling. Eventually you come to your senses and wonder about yourself and the situation. You question your behavior but are intoxicated by the thrill of the experience. You are in over your head and the future is now undetermined.

Katie's Story

Katie didn't consider herself naive and she never thought herself capable of cheating on her husband, Todd. But she did feel the distance between them growing each day. She felt lonely, isolated and sad. She didn't have anything bad to say about her husband apart from the fact that they had drifted apart. She was at a loss to figure out how to bring them closer together. Both were heavily involved with work and volunteer activities and both kept very different schedules.

One day, feeling particularly down, Katie left a simple message on her online page: "Feeling lonely."

Bob sent Katie a private message asking, "What's wrong?" Katie didn't really know anything about Bob. He had "friended" her one day as a friend of a friend. He was, however, the first to pick up on her sign of distress.

Katie, not really looking for a response after flagging her emotional state, at first ignored Bob's message. Bob, not receiving a reply within the day, followed up with, "Sorry if I was too forward. Just thought you needed a friend." This endeared him to Katie. He appeared intuitive and thoughtful.

She readily replied with a vague message telling him that she had a trying day. He didn't push but demonstrated empathy by saying he'd had days like that too. His non-aggressive style prompted Katie to say more. He seemed safe. She confided that she felt herself distancing from her husband and was forlorn because of the situation. Bob reflected back to her the sentiment she expressed, but took it a step further by saying it hurt to feel detached from someone who should be special.

Katie felt that Bob understood her emotions. This endeared him more to her and soon they began chatting about all sorts of things: the weather, recreational activities and work-related problems. Katie began to believe they were kindred spirits.

Katie and Bob's messaging continued and intensified. Within a matter of a few weeks they were chatting back and forth on many subjects. Katie was freely telling Bob how oblivious her husband was to her distress and how disengaged they were as a couple. Rather than forlorn, Katie sounded merely factual, as if she had come to view her current status with her husband as the new normal.

There was a sense of freedom that accompanied Katie's online chatting as well as a seemingly renewed sense of adventure. Katie sought to explore mutual interests with Bob. They both enjoyed hiking and so she thought they might take an afternoon together and go for a walk by the bay. Innocent enough, although when Katie reflected on her impressions of Bob, she realized she knew little of him. She comforted herself with thoughts about how intuitive and supportive he was.

Katie and Bob met quietly and discreetly to go for their walk together. Bob behaved as a perfect gentleman and looked every bit the likeness of his online pictures.

When departing, Bob extended his hand to Katie's arm. He held his hand on her arm, said goodbye and they both walked back to their cars. Katie was awakened. Katie was alarmed. She repeated to herself, *a touch is just a touch.* Secretly she thought it meant more and she felt both shameful and excited.

Katie was reluctant to sign into her social media page for a few days following her walk with Bob. She wondered what he felt as the result of his touch. I didn't brush it off, she thought. I didn't object, she thought. They had politely said goodbye and went their separate ways, yet Katie wondered what Bob was thinking.

After a few days of waiting and wondering, Katie went online. It turned out Bob was away on a trip. Thinking little of it, apart from teasing herself about the intrigue of his touch, Katie returned to thinking about her husband Todd. Guilt set in. Katie wrestled with the fact she had developed a special, secretive relationship with a man outside of her primary intimate partnership. She remembered how she and her husband used to hike together and how that used to be one of their favorite shared activities. Katie began to mourn the loss of closeness with her husband and felt compelled to do something about it.

Katie planned to talk with Todd on an evening she knew he would be available. Unbeknownst to him, she remained home one evening when he thought she had another engagement. Unsure of why Katie was there when he returned home, he asked why she was home. Katie extended her invitation to talk with her husband about feeling distanced.

Todd, not really having the chance to prepare for such a conversation, was reserved. He didn't know what to say and was somewhat taken aback. There was little he could offer apart from validating Katie's view that they weren't as close anymore. He also seemed somewhat irritable hearing about their problems and not knowing what to do about it. Katie suggested counseling and her husband agreed. It did register with him that she was quite distressed about their relationship and, realizing this was more than he had imagined, he wondered if there were other issues beyond his awareness.

Todd began snooping on Katie's computer and quickly found and read the chat history between her and Bob. Immediately he came to the conclusion Katie was having an affair. He was furious and felt vengeful.

We tell our children not to play with fire, but the spark of the match tempts with the promise of a flame. Katie was at first unsuspecting but soon enticed. The match was struck, but the flame extinguished before fully igniting. There was the promise of heat, but Katie managed to step back before things got out of hand.

Katie's husband, however, saw the spark. While Katie kept matters from alighting, her husband already felt burned.

Asking when an affair is an affair reminds me of an old *Seinfeld* episode where Elaine asks Jerry when he considers sex to have taken place. Jerry replies, "When the nipple makes its first appearance." With regard to an affair, while Katie and Bob didn't have sex by Jerry's definition, do you think Katie's husband felt the same way about it? The nipple didn't make an appearance, so was this an affair?

For many like Katie, an affair is a slippery slope and, for many women, it is not the pursuit of sex that entices but the emotional connection with a kindred spirit. Loneliness, a need to feel valued and a fragile self-esteem all breed vulnerability. But where do these issues come from? What gives rise to them such that someone could be vulnerable to the likes of an affair?

FEELING VALUED

There are two key ingredients to healthy self-esteem. The first is to be valued by our parents. I used to say that evidence of being valued by parents began at birth, then I came to believe it started in utero during the mother's pregnancy, but now I believe that evidence of being valued by one's parents begins in mate selection. Yes, the healthy self-esteem of our offspring begins with our choice of partner.

If we anticipate having children one day, then our choice of partner should be determined not just by our fanciful attraction, but also with some degree of forethought around matters of ongoing compatibility, financial stability, mutual respect, decency of behavior and ability to resolve conflict peacefully. An intended mate should be reasonably healthy physically, mentally and spiritually. To whatever degree a mate is not healthy, there should be consideration and dis-cussion as to how the issue, whatever it is, will be handled so as to per-mit for the reasonable care and raising of a child. Your future child's self-esteem hinges very much on your mate selection and the ability of you and your partner to focus on the needs of the child ahead of your own during any issues that may arise.

Assuming reasonable mate selection, the issue of valuing extends to prenatal maternal health during pregnancy. The soon-to-be mother takes care of her health and this priority is supported by her partner. Maternal drug, alcohol and tobacco use normally ceases during the period of pregnancy. The relationship remains peaceful and the needs of the budding mother are reasonably attended to.

Together, mate selection and maternal health and well-being during pregnancy signal to the developing spirit that he or she is val-ued. Why else would persons so consider their choices and behavior if not to advance the needs of their intended offspring?

Then the expectant parents prepare for delivery and the subse-quent care of their little one. The baby arrives with much anticipation and preparation. The child is swathed, cleaned, fed and nurtured. These parental behaviors again signal to the child that he or she is valued.

As the child continues to grow, it is well cared for. When the child cries to signal a need, the good parent seeks to understand the need. Is it a dirty diaper, hunger or a need for soothing, entertainment and stimulation? As the child grows, its achievements are met with plea-sure and praise: she holds her head up now; he is sitting up; she is crawling; he is walking; she said her first words. The parents celebrate their child's advances with love, praise and adoration.

As parents continue in these loving, caring parental behaviors, they continue to signal to their child that he or she is of value, is wanted, is special and has a place in their hearts and in the world. In so doing, the child comes to internalize this sense of worth we call self-esteem. The child comes to know he or she is of value through these parental behaviors. The child, feeling secure within him or her-self, develops a belief that he or she has a place in the world, belongs in the world and can function in the world. With that sense of value, the child becoming an adult can set out into the world as a confident person, able to take on the tasks of adult living.

COMPETENCY

The second key ingredient to healthy self-esteem is a sense of competency. Competency refers to an ability to manipulate the world so one might meet one's needs. Here the word *manipulate* has no negative connotations. Manipulation in this sense is a good thing. It means one satisfies or satiates a need. For instance, as the infant learns to creep and crawl, the infant is manipulating his body and is satisfying a need to ambulate—to get from one point in space to another. As the toddler learns to walk, the child can get from one place to another quicker and easier without wearing out his knees on the carpet or flooring. As the infant, seated in the high chair, puts her fingers in a bowl of mash and draws her fingers from the bowl to her mouth, she satiates her hunger. As the toddler learns language, he can more easily express his needs and wants verbally. To the degree to which children learn and develop these competencies and satisfy their own needs, they feel good about themselves. Before long children take pride in dressing themselves, saying, "I'll do it!" They learn to manipulate things in their environment and take care of themselves. When appropriately guided, children also learn to take care of themselves at no one else's expense, such that social relationships are respected. Children not only develop physical competencies, but social competencies as well. They take care of themselves in such a manner that they impose no harm on another.

Thus we have these two major ingredients to healthy self-esteem: feeling valued and being competent, meeting our needs at no one else's expense.

POOR SELF-ESTEEM

Unfortunately, though, not every child feels valued and not every child develops an ability to meet his or her needs at no one else's expense.

Indeed, some children's parents should never have been together and should never have co-produced offspring. Some parents cannot provide for sensible prenatal maternal health or children's needs upon birth. For periods of time during their rearing the children's needs are not met on a reasonable basis.

Some children are unwanted or raised by a parent or parents whose desire to have and care for the child is tempered by ambivalence, the kind of ambivalence that transfers through the care of the child right to the child's sense of being valued. Some parents' inability to support each other and/or resolve conflict peacefully results in children being raised in emotional and physical war zones. Some children are the battlegrounds for parental disputes, some children are used solely for the inappropriate gratification of a parent and yet other children are left unprotected from exploitation by others or with inadequate supervision or guidance to keep them safe or lead them wisely. In these less-than-adequate situations, what of the child's need to feel valued? How does a child in undeserving, inadequate or marginal circumstances develop a sense of self-worth? How is this child's need to be valued satisfied and what if it isn't?

Being valued is not only every child's birthright, but also a biologically determined need that must be satisfied, just like hunger and thirst. Those who grow up being reasonably valued generally fare better in the world than those who do not. Being valued leads to a better chance of survival.

UNSATISFIED NEEDS

Just like not having eaten for the day leads to a physical hunger that must be satiated, so too does an unsatisfied need to be valued require resolution. The degree to which we are not valued by our parents leads us to be emotionally needy, seeking something to satisfy that hunger. We see this phenomenon in those who overeat, drink to excess, become hooked on drugs or seek other dysfunctional strategies for filling emotional holes. We also see this phenomenon in people subject to affairs, particularly women. This speaks to the question of why women are drawn into affairs, why they need and seek emotional connections and how they are vulnerable to something which they might otherwise feel shameful for participating in. There is inner turmoil, particularly in women, between satiating a grumbling unmet need for being valued and validated as a person versus maintaining the fidelity of their primary intimate relationships.

Sadly, when starved enough, we might be convinced to eat anything. We lose our presence of mind and our thinking becomes distorted as we deny our behavior or rationalize away deeds we would never undertake given the best of circumstances.

Katie's vulnerability to an affair clouded her judgment. She was enticed into a relationship by a seemingly caring man. Her vulnerability was heightened by unmet or poorly met needs of her own, thus far unrealized by her. She needed to learn where her needs came from, how to make her needs reasonably known to her husband and how to manage meeting her needs in a functional way so that she would no longer be vulnerable to behavior that only served to undermine her well-being and jeopardize further her already shaky sense of self-worth.

SELF ESTEEM VERSUS SELF-RIGHTEOUSNESS

As we've discussed, the other key ingredient to healthy self-esteem is the development of competency, not just physical or academic competencies but social competencies too. Healthy self-esteem requires an ability to meet one's needs through manipulating the world or the objects within and around oneself at no one else's expense. In this sense, self-esteem is distinguished from self-righteousness. Self-righteousness also implies an attitude about one's self, but the self-righteous go about meeting their needs with little to no concern about others. As the self-righteous seek to satisfy their needs, this can include meeting their needs over the needs of others and even at the expense of others.

To the person who is self-righteous, meeting one's needs is an end unto itself. There is a sense of entitlement that is part of the persona of the self-righteous. Not having had the need to be valued met, the self-righteous do not consider others to be of value in their own right. In the absence of having their need to be valued appropriately met, coupled with learning that one can pursue one's needs at the expense of others, the self-righteous appear to have little or no conscience—little or no concern about the impact of their behavior on the well-being of another. The self-righteous have their own mantra: I deserve to have my needs met as I see fit and I have learned how to do so with little to no concern for your welfare. I can manipulate the world and those in it to serve myself.

As the self-righteous set out to meet their needs, they may be unsophisticated and obvious in their approaches or you may not see them coming, yet be devastated by the outcome.

To Katie, Bob appeared the savior for her loneliness, but was he really the decent man he appeared to be? Bob was able to key in on Katie's sad feelings and reflect some degree of understanding. Bob thus endeared himself to Katie. But was this altruistic? Was this truly an effort to act in Katie's interest?

SEX AND INTIMACY

Bob was aware that Katie was married. Would you not think that a reasonable and well-adjusted person could easily surmise that a secret meeting, no matter how innocent, would be a cause for concern for one's partner? Was Bob's kind and caring outward manner his true self or was it like the lure to the prey? Was his outward manner the shiny object with which to catch the object of his desire to satisfy his own needs?

Women are sexual creatures, but while they typically are motivated by a desire for emotional intimacy, men are more sexually motivated. For many women, sex is an expression of the emotional intimacy already achieved; intimacy leads to sex. For many men, sex is an end; sex may lead to intimacy. For men, sex feels great as a function of the orgasm; for women, it's the sense of closeness, even though they can and do enjoy the orgasm. Stereotypical, perhaps, but accurate in general.

Not all women are motivated solely by a desire for intimacy and some men have emotional intimacy as a primary objective too. Some women, like many men, are motivated by only a desire for sexual gratification. However, women are more likely to seek emotional intimacy first and then a sexual relationship becomes a benefit of that relationship, whereas men are more likely to seek sex first and thereafter develop an attachment leading to an exclusive sexual and intimate relationship.

No truly caring man would put a married woman or a woman currently in a relationship in a position of conflict with her partner. It is not a loving or caring act to develop a clandestine relationship, a relationship that by definition develops outside the awareness of that woman's partner.

VULNERABILITY

Bob, by facilitating Katie's attraction to him, contributed to the divide she experienced with her husband. This intensified Katie and Todd's marital problems and created greater conflict, even if beyond her husband's awareness. Bob wasn't innocent. Bob's caring was nothing more than a shiny lure, bait. He was patient. He trolled slowly.

Katie knew little of Bob, but she thought he was intuitive and supportive. Bob knew how to stalk his prey. Go for the weak; go for the vulnerable. Take your time; build rapport and trust. He portrayed himself well. However, all the while Bob was allowing Katie to move deeper and deeper into the trap.

From Katie's perspective, she saw herself as a willing, active, if not leading, character in the development of this promising relationship. The allure of satisfying unmet needs of feeling valued and being validated as a person, as a woman, was at stake. Bob not only set the trap, but also, by taking his time and allowing Katie to walk her way into it, he cemented a perspective that it was she who initiated a move to further impropriety, thus creating the impression that Bob was still a decent and caring man.

Bob created the impression in Katie that she was fully to blame for the meeting, walk and touch that occurred between them. Bob could claim that he had not asked Katie to go out together. Now that is masterful manipulation. Dangle a lure to the unsuspecting and vulnerable, draw the prey in on the pull of seeking to satiate its own vulnerability, its own hunger, set the bait with the tease of partial satisfaction and then sit back as the prey jumps in with both feet of its own accord so the predator can look innocent just as it ensnares the prey.

This isn't meant to be a guide on how a self-serving man can lure a vulnerable woman. No, this book is intended to make the dynamics of certain human behavior more understandable so that partners who are experiencing marital distress can better understand how they get into these situations in order to keep out of them in the future. Katie was in a situation created with stealth and manipulation by Bob. She was caused to feel like the primary actor, decision maker and leader, but this occurred because a man took advantage of her vulnerability for his personal gratification.

To be enticed into an affair is not a loving act, is not an act of kindness, is not an act of benevolence; it is an act of self-righteous, egocentric interest. It is an abuse of trust by another person to serve his or her own interest. It is abuse in that it further undermines what should be a sacred relationship with a significant other—one's marital partner.

AFFAIRS AND VALUES

An affair abuses one's spiritual self and relationship with a higher power, if one's beliefs include a higher power. If the subject of the affair also has children, the affair wreaks havoc on that person's relationship with his or her children. It undermines the person's view of him or herself as a moral role model who must lead his or her children through adolescence, which includes developing, learning about and managing social and special relationships. And if or when a child has difficulty in a relationship, what will the parent as a role model of infidelity provide as an example?

While there are always those who say their current relationships began as affairs and they work well for them, for the vast majority, this situation does not. Of those who extol the virtue of relationships that began as affairs, their tune quite often changes. And if they show favor toward their affairs, then ask them to look beyond their immediate selves to the social ripples cast from the relationships made of their affairs. Are their other relationships intact? Do they all get along well with their parents? Is their relationship fully accepted by all? Do their children speak to them? Has the prior spouse/partner moved on or is this other person still recovering from the loss of a sacred trust, a trust gone awry? All too often people delude themselves that relationships begun as affairs are wholesome and without lasting consequences. Upon closer scrutiny this is rarely the case but may appear so to the actors within, whose fragile senses of themselves require more limited visions of success.

When a partner goes on to cheat again, this time on you, should you really be surprised? The best predictor of future behavior is prior behavior, particularly if the prior behavior has not been addressed and has not been remediated. It is a terrible fall from grace when a person who entered a relationship based on an affair loses that relationship based on yet another affair, this one perpetrated against that person. As the saying goes, fool me once, shame on you; fool me twice, shame on me.

BOUNDARY VIOLATIONS

In social work and clinical jargon, we speak about boundaries and boundary violations. Marriages and monogamous relationships are held together by invisible boundaries. Spouses are in the circle of fidelity. They do not stray from each other with respect to this circle, this boundary of fidelity. The circle doesn't extend just to their sexual selves, but to their emotional selves too. There is something special about the relationship, for why else should people even consider themselves to be in a relationship? What is it that makes this so special?

In a marriage or intimate monogamous relationship, that specialness is the expectation of not just sexual but emotional fidelity, and partners prioritize each other for the maintenance of the relationship. Emotional fidelity is about that special feeling that comes from a place of shared expectations, shared positive feelings toward each other, shared dreams and hopes, shared but otherwise private points of view special to the couple because they are to be kept between the partners—within the boundary. Partners maintain the boundary, because without it there is nothing to keep them together. When partners are stretched and the boundary is at risk of tearing, they run toward the weakened area, toward the breach, seeking to repair it. To repair such a weakened area partners must discuss, reflect and, when necessary, accommodate and alter behavior in order to maintain the integrity of the boundary. They sort things out with each other. An affair is the antithesis of maintaining the boundary of sexual or emotional fidelity.

Those who would walk down the path of impropriety, stretching the boundaries of their fidelity, may argue, "But it wasn't sexual. We did not have sex." Their language may couch a transgression and for those who truly had no physical contact, they righteously argue that nothing happened in a physical context. Yet their defensive posture betrays the fact that they strayed emotionally; that the specialness of a relationship that was to be reserved for one's partner was diverted to another. This person is trying desperately to maintain the illusion of a personal boundary in order to be perceived as having individual integrity, lest they be shamed. The more one defends one's transgression, the deeper the transgression becomes as behaviors of deceit are compounded.

TWO TYPES OF AFFAIRS

We distinguish between two types of affairs: sexual and emotional. Straying emotionally, redirecting one's special feelings, those meant for one's significant other, onto someone else, is an affair, a breach of the boundary of who partners are as a couple. Some will take exception to the idea that stepping out on one's partner emotionally qualifies as an affair. Those who do may be struggling to assuage their own feelings of guilt that might bring disrepute or further injury to an already fragile sense of self-worth.

Katie entered into therapy with her husband, Todd, who was reeling from the realization that his wife had strayed emotionally. He was flooded with feelings ranging from betrayal to loss to anger to sadness and, oddly enough, even joy in view of the fact that the misery of their distanced marriage might be repaired.

However, overcome with the intensity of his bad feelings, it was difficult for him to remain positive and to be kind in the moment to Katie. Her husband was not abusive, but he was holding back his emotions that, if unleashed, he feared would destroy Katie. His holding back was meant to be constructive, yet Katie interpreted it as passive-aggressive withholding—the intentional withholding of feelings with the aim to destabilize Katie's sense of emotional security. She didn't know where she stood with Todd. She felt she deserved his anger and upset, but nothing was forthcoming. She felt like she was in limbo, not knowing his thoughts or feelings. Can he forgive me? she wondered.

This intensified Katie's sense of uncertainty, driving her to greater discomfort. Should Katie use the feelings her husband generated in her as evidence to the therapist that Todd was not a good man?

The therapist had to support both Katie and Todd emotionally without dismissing or minimizing Katie's emotional affair, but also without causing her to feel worse than she did already. The therapist had to help Katie to understand her unique vulnerability and how it was exploited beyond her awareness, but in a way that did not preclude her taking some responsibility for her choices.

The therapist sought to normalize the feelings of both persons in view of the issues before them. It was hard not to focus just on the emotional affair as that alone crystallized one partner as bad and the other as the victim of the breach of fidelity. The affair became the sticking point and the ability to step back and take a broader perspective was a challenge. The therapist began by facilitating Todd's expression of his bad feelings.

"How could you?" He emoted.

And Katie responded, "I didn't mean to."

Todd repeated, "How could you?" Katie gave the same response again.

This is the dance of blame and guilt that, if not expanded upon, will only serve as the sabre of a couple's divide. Given the intensity of pain in the moment, it is difficult to see past the dance. In some cases the therapist allows the dance to continue, hoping to "bleed off" some of the intensity; that the catharsis, pouring out of intense emotions, might release some of the pain so that the couple can then place attention on the matters of their relationship that gave rise to the breach in the first place.

This can be a challenging intervention for the therapist. Some couples only escalate their bad feelings instead of experiencing relief. Intended catharsis can backfire. The therapist makes this calculated move recognizing that the couple could become stuck and weighs that alternative against the risk of escalating the intensity of the spouses' bad feelings.

With a break in Todd's outpouring of emotion, the therapist in-terjected and commented upon how his negative feelings were, at the same time, an indication of his love for Katie, for why else would this be so consequential? Todd felt understood; he got back in touch with caring for Katie.

For Katie, Todd's feelings of love for her were strangely com-forting and validating—the very essence of what she sought in her relationship with him.

Then the therapist helped this couple step back to examine fully the larger context of their relationship, including their per-sonal histories that may have contributed to the vulnerabilities of the present.

One of the greatest challenges for Katie was coming to understand Bob's behavior. Katie, to some degree, was still en-ticed by Bob. She thought of him in positive terms, believing it was she alone who transgressed, that it was she, without ma-nipulation, who generated the idea to go for a walk together.

She continued to view Bob as providing what she wanted most from her husband, that sense of worth and validation. It took much reflection on Katie's part, with the guidance of the therapist, to see that Bob wasn't so innocent and supportive, given that he knowingly participated in, if not manipulatively created, a situation that could never be in the larger interest of Katie's well-being. Bob's involvement with Katie subverted the sanctity and fidelity of her marriage, escalated her conflict with her husband and undermined her spirituality.

Affairs of the nature of Bob and Katie's are actually a form of psychological abuse. Bob's deft maneuvers created in Katie a dis-torted view of the situation, causing her to think he was loving and caring. He played with her mind, against her interests and toward his own gratification. To repeat from earlier, no loving and caring person would put someone else in such a position of conflict so as to cause that person harm. An affair creates conflict and harm. The only questions that remain after the affair ends are: Can the conflicts be resolved? Can the harm be undone?

SPIRITUAL CONFLICT

Additionally, the situation with Bob created an internal conflict for Katie as she had to wrestle not only with feelings of shame but also conflicts of a spiritual nature regardless of her religious beliefs or affiliation. Just by being raised in society one is aware of and internalizes to some extent the value of remaining monogamous and not committing adultery.

Regardless if Katie understands how she was lured in and taken advantage of, she still must reconcile her behavior against her vows of fidelity and against what is a sacred trust in any committed relationship. What if she was religious? The spiritual wound imposed by her behavior could cause her to feel unworthy in the eyes of her faith as well as in the community.

Though the therapist was able to help Katie begin to repair her relationship with her husband, the therapist couldn't repair Katie's spiritual wound. Katie was a lapsed Catholic who, although lapsed, still felt damned. The therapist, recognizing Katie's spiritual distress and her ties with her religion, suggested that Katie visit a priest and seek confession and absolution. The therapist explained that this part of her distress was not an intellectual issue. This matter was spiritual.

Katie did decide to see a priest and went through the process of confession. The experience reminded her of her childhood. She recalled how she never really liked attending Church, feeling hypocritical given what transpired in her home during the week. It didn't match the image her family presented at Church on Sunday.

*Through the process of returning to her religion and through
confession, Katie came to realize that she confused her upset at
her family's hypocrisy with the role and function of her Church.
Now she was able to separate her family from her spirituality
and the Church and she no longer blamed the Church for issues
originating with her family. She experienced relief having con-
fessed that she, in stretching the boundary of her marriage on
an emotional basis, had created a type of infidelity for which
she felt bad. This also resolved the dilemma of not being fully
responsible for what had occurred between her and Bob, yet still
being responsible for acting in a manner that brought harm to
her marriage.*

*Katie did not become a religious Catholic as the result of
this experience, but her disdain for the Church disappeared and
the role of spirituality as a valid and important part of her life
was reawakened. It caused her to act with greater resolve to address future issues with her husband more forthrightly. Whereas
Katie hadn't felt valued as a child, her self-supportive behavior
and connection with her spiritual self created in her a belief that
she was finally a worthwhile human being. This boded well for
the integrity of her marriage in the future.*

EXAMINING BOB'S BEHAVIOR

But what of Bob? Consider the key ingredients of which we've been
talking in addition to healthy self-esteem. Healthy self-esteem means
you feel good at no one's expense; it is relational in that you can feel
good and this can be mutual and in the collective interest. It includes
social competencies and learning how to resolve conflict peacefully
in the interest of all parties. Healthy self-esteem leads to altruistic
behavior—behavior that is motivated in the best interests of others—
and doesn't allow for hurting others.

All of this is contrasted with self-righteousness, a feeling of deserving but with little or no concern as to the needs or well-being of others. The self-righteous have a sense of entitlement and they seek their objectives with different degrees of ability and sophistication. Therefore, while one may appear awkward and obvious, another may be surreptitious yet will still wreak havoc. Bob wreaked havoc in the most insidious of ways, presenting himself as caring and supportive but undermining Katie's sense of self, her marriage and her spirituality. Bob can rationally state that he did nothing wrong. He didn't ask Katie for a walk; indeed he was supposedly just acting kindly.

If we could examine Bob's upbringing, it is likely that his father treated his mother poorly, was controlling and punitive, looked out for himself first before all others and viewed winning as of greater importance than sportsmanship.

The likes of Bob are seen less frequently in therapy. Their attitude of self-righteousness and sense of entitlement precludes them from viewing themselves in critical terms. When they do enter therapy, it is usually at the urging of someone else who is distressed by their behavior. Therapy may only be constructive if they see an advantage for themselves greater than the advantage for the other. People like Bob can be satisfying to some as partners, as long as their needs and interests are fulfilled first. At that point it doesn't cost that person anything or there may be some other perceived gain for the person unbeknownst to the partner.

While it would be nice to see Bob and those like him reform and improve their ways, the likelihood is limited. They are more apt to play victims than conspirators. These types are available in abundance through social media.

SOCIAL MEDIA

Social media, chat rooms, video chat rooms and other online sites are the breeding grounds for the exploration and sourcing of adulterous relationships. Social media in this context is anything but social. It might best be considered anti-social when one considers the harm these sites wreak on partners, extended kin, children and friends. This is by no means an indictment of social media in its totality, as social media does provide useful, non-injurious functions. Social media keeps us connected with family and friends, allows for the teaching of skills across distances, facilitates assessment and treatment of people who otherwise could not access healthcare services and allows for multiple inputs toward the greater development of shared objectives. Social media can be and is a great thing, except when its use subverts the interests of others and, in the context of this book, the fidelity of a couple's relationship.

When does a relationship with an online friend or any other kind of friend become an affair? It occurs when you flirt with behavior that would entice you away from and undermine the sanctity of your primary intimate relationship. If your partner accepts that you had an emotional affair, then your partner is telling you that you have crossed the line.

If you went online with interest or exploration and without your partner's awareness, you have indeed crossed the line. This behavior will never serve your relationship. The excuse of making something good after the bad is a sorrowful one. It may be better than nothing, but if harm can be prevented in the first place, this is better. The fewer emotional assaults we endure over the course of our lives, the healthier we can be. This is not to say we don't want to repair harm done and create something better from the bad, but why create more turmoil when we can address our partners beforehand, before we bring greater harm to the relationship and then try to improve matters. It behooves people in challenging relationships to seek help before falling prey to exacerbating strategies. If you have already erred, then for the sake of your personal integrity and the sanctity of your relationship, address your wrong as well as the issues leading up to it.

TRANSGRESSIONS AND REPAIRS

Your wife or husband may have transgressed against you or you may have transgressed against your spouse. It's time to repair. The affair must come to an end. There is no way to feel good about oneself or to fix a failing marriage in the context of an ongoing affair. The fallout from ending the adulterous relationship may be immense. The person with whom you had an affair may seek vengeance. You may feel this person's wrath, be it in the name of revenge, spite or the belief it can somehow maintain your wrongful relationship.

It is best to anticipate a forceful backlash when news of the affair comes out. Many people teeter on the fulcrum of disclosure versus nondisclosure. There is no one best approach here. Each situation must be assessed on its own merits. I only caution that if you choose nondisclosure, it's not just to save yourself. Nondisclosure is best considered in the context of the well-being of the partner, but nondisclosure will mean an inauthentic existence for yourself. You will always have that secret between you and your spouse.

If you don't know what to do, then seek guidance. Meet with a counselor who can help you explore your situation more fully to facilitate a more well-rounded decision. Even if you do see the merit of disclosure, you may wish to consult a counselor to determine the most constructive manner for doing so. Be aware that counseling, though, cannot be a place to hide. Counseling must be goal directed to help you produce an outcome or a process by which action can be taken. To sit and navel gaze only provides the illusion of taking responsibility and seeking change; it actually serves the function of delaying action.

FREEING ONESELF

Assuming your partner discovers the affair, whether because you confess or through the report of another, be prepared to take responsibility unreservedly. Even if you were enticed by crafty manipulation or unresolved issues from your past, you broke the boundary. You are not taking a one-sided responsibility for all the issues in the marriage, only for your participation with respect to the affair. Admitting wrong is both frightening and freeing. The freeing part may not be felt for some time, but the owning of one's behavior, even in wrongdoing, breeds respect in the long run. It causes one to appear conscientious and is emotionally liberating. This assumes you are not self-righteous in your disclosure but that your disclosure is based on expressing guilt and genuine remorse.

With regard to the concept of restorative justice, we seek to have the perpetrator of harm take responsibility for the misdeed directly with the victim. We want the perpetrator to appreciate the harm imposed upon the victim and to seek restitution by some act meant to restore the situation. In so doing, the perpetrator learns about the impact of his or her behavior upon another, corrects for it and creates the conditions for forgiveness by the victim. Through the process, the victim can become a survivor and the perpetrator can become reformed. In the best of these situations, the survivor and the reformed develop a respectful appreciation for each other. This is the objective in taking responsibility for an affair.

Many affairs are suspected by partners, but the perpetrators may be deceptive if confronted. The illusive behavior of the adulterer may cause the partner to question his or her own judgment. For some, as this process proceeds, the partner comes to experience depression and/or anxiety, feeling he or she cannot rely on his or her own reasonable view of reality. The lies and subterfuge create mental health issues for the partner. Taking responsibility, even at this late stage and even if met with extreme anger, releases the partner from thinking he or she was crazy in swallowing the deception. While you are hurting your partner with the truth in the moment, you are acting to restore his or her view of his or her own judgment. "You were right all along. I was having an affair. I lied and caused you to question your judgment. For that, I am truly sorry."

Taking responsibility is the first step to recovery from an affair. For many couples that is as far as they get. The affair is admitted but the hurt is never really resolved. They become stuck in the revolving door of "when/how will I know I can trust you?" Their marriages remain conflicted and unsatisfying. Other couples go on to explore the conditions that led to the affair. Along the way to a true recovery, couples must address the issue of trust.

RESTORING TRUST

Trust is not achieved or granted based on a confession or on a promise of non-adulterous behavior. Trust can only be an outcome of transparent and accountable behavior over the course of time.

While such behavior can be subject to questions and manipulation, one still must pursue transparency and accountability. The offending partner must make his or her whereabouts known to the other partner at all times. Further, computer use should be in an open area and passwords must be known to the partner. Internet browser history and chat history must always be intact and accessible. Assuming you no longer have anything to hide, then don't hide anything. This is not to be construed as being controlled by your partner, but to demonstrate your openness to scrutiny and accountability. You have transgressed and an affair means you kept secrets and lied, even if only the lie of omission. You must take steps to remedy the untoward image you created for yourself in order to restore your partner's trust in your behavior and faith in your word.

How long it takes to restore trust and how long this new normal should continue is difficult to say. It should take as long as necessary with these new systems of accountability and transparency. Truly intact, well-functioning marriages have such transparency and accountability. If you say you are going to be home at a certain time, then do so. Your actions must be congruent with your stated intentions. If you are going to be late, call your spouse and let him or her know. Why should your partner be inconvenienced with worry about your late arrival? That is inconsiderate. With this behavior, over time your spouse may come to respect your word and relax into the relationship. Then the tension from before, made worse by the affair, can dissipate.

In my marriage, my wife can rely on me to follow through as stated or requested and I am accountable. She is welcome to sit at my computer and see all the files and histories on it, because I have nothing to hide and I am transparent. Because we are open with each other, neither of us has any real need to question or survey. This is as a good relationship should be. This is what you are striving for in repairing your own.

For many partners, an affair is a much more difficult circumstance to overcome than alcoholism, drug abuse or even assault. It may be that without the bond of fidelity there is no basis for a relationship.

FIXING FIDELITY'S BOND

If that bond of fidelity has been stretched, crossed or broken, address it and fix it. Given the seriousness of this issue, there is no guarantee that your relationship will endure. The fallout may be greater than ever anticipated. An affair can sever one's relationship not only with one's spouse, but also with one's kin, one's children and one's community. Repair will be a process over time with many impediments along the way. It will require both partners to examine their contributions to marital dissatisfaction and take steps to remediate. The challenge throughout will be in maintaining reasonable behavior amid the intensity of anguish and other negative feelings.

In addition to the emotional, spiritual and relationship work, if the affair has extended to a sexually intimate encounter of any kind, then you must concern yourself with your sexual health. It behooves you and your partner to get testing for AIDS as well as all other sexually transmitted infections. Some sexual infections lay dormant and without symptoms. Feeling well is not necessarily an indication of perfect health. For women in particular, some sexual infections can give rise to infertility—to be discovered at a later date and then traced back to the indiscretion.

You may try to tell yourself that you were your lover's only tryst or you may have believed it when that person claimed he or she was sexually healthy, yet you are in an affair. Affairs are illicit, based on secrecy and deception, and you simply cannot trust the other person's reported sexual health. You will never know another person's sexual history with 100 percent certainty. Get yourself tested. Your partner must be tested too. Just because you have negative test results doesn't mean that you still couldn't have passed an infection on to your partner. You must be responsible for the sake of your health and that of your partner. It will be another hardship between you and him or her, perhaps an embarrassment, yet this is one vital way you can take responsibility for your decisions and your actions.

If you do the work, if you reflect on your contribution to distress and cooperate with your partner to restore a wholesome relationship, the benefits can be tremendous. If you have children, they will then be in a home where the parents model how to overcome adversity with personal responsibility. This will bode well for your children as they become adults dealing with their own problems and issues along life's path.

The Winner's Motto:
I am reserved for my partner only.

Abusing Alcohol or Drugs

The Sinner's Motto:
I can quit anytime I want.

Alcohol consumption has caused the end of many good relationships. People can provide many excuses and rationales for the amount of alcohol they consume; however, the more a person consumes, the less that person is available emotionally and sometimes physically and financially to meet the needs of others.

People have their own ideas about what constitutes an alcoholic. Here are some stories of men and women who imbibe alcohol. Are they alcoholics?

Annabella's Story

For Annabella and her husband Andy, pregnancy occasioned marriage. They wed in high school. Annabella had to give up her plans for college. She had wanted to be a veterinary assistant, but then she gave birth to her first daughter, Serita. She and Andy made a joint decision that she would be a stay-at-home mom. When Serita was two, Annabella became pregnant again and soon Jocelyn entered the family. Two years later, Andy and Annabella had their third daughter, Teresa.

As she tried to cope with the care of her three children, Annabella realized she couldn't manage more. Annabella decided she needed assurance that she wouldn't become pregnant again. She considered having a tubal ligation, but since she was only twenty-five, her doctor was reluctant to oblige.

As time passed she grew terrified at the thought of having another baby, of another year of breastfeeding, of another child to place demands on her. She broached the subject of a vasectomy with her husband. However, Andy's sense of manhood was tied to his virility and he refused. But as Annabella grew more hostile about the issue, their intimate life began to fade away. Finally Andy decided he would agree to have the vasectomy. They began to have sexual relations again, although never like they used to at the start of their relationship.

Something had changed in Annabella; a quiet resentment overcame her. It intruded upon everything she did. Her emotional availability diminished. She wasn't as responsive to her husband or the girls as she used to be.

Annabella found that she needed time for herself, but the time she took for herself coincided with the exact time her girls got off the bus after school. It was then that Annabella sat in the kitchen, in the chair everyone knew was hers. She was not to be disturbed while seated there. That chair represented her alone time, her quiet space. She sipped a drink she told the children was tea. But Annabella's tea consisted of one part gin and one part vermouth. She only ever had one cup of this brew in a sitting, enjoyed daily, precisely upon the girls' arrival home from school.

One particular day, Annabella's daughter Serita, who was nine at the time, came bouncing into the house announcing the "A" she had received on a very difficult assignment. Serita was looking for her mother's approval and praise. Annabella reminded Serita that this was Annabella's private time and suggested, as she sipped her "tea," that she could look at Serita's assignment later, after dinner. Silently, Serita took her work upstairs to place in a drawer.

On another day, Jocelyn, then age seven, came sullenly through the kitchen at the end of a school day to tell her mother she had been bullied at school by a girl Jocelyn had thought was her friend. But the other girl had been secretly making fun of Jocelyn to their classmates. Jocelyn had barely begun her story when Annabella reminded Jocelyn, as she had Serita, that this was her mother's private time and Jocelyn should tell her after dinner. Later that day, when Annabella approached Jocelyn after dinner to catch up on Jocelyn's story, Jocelyn told her mother it wasn't really anything important.

Teresa, the youngest daughter, had her account too, which happened when she was five years old. As she was bounding up the cement stairs to enter the house upon her return from school, she tripped and hit her knee against the edge of the top step. There was no gushing blood, no broken bones and only a small red scratch. But to little Teresa, the injury was a trauma. Teresa entered the house crying and clutching her knee as she walked awkwardly toward her mother. Annabella, rather than helping to clean and bandage the tiny injury, reminded Teresa that her mother was not to be disturbed and sent her on her way, shouting to Serita to take care of her younger sister. Serita, at nine years old, had long since been comforting Teresa. Meanwhile, Annabella continued to sip her cup of "tea."

Annabella has only one drink daily, yet it occurs at precisely the time her children are likely to need her. Annabella's marriage is intact; the girls are fed, sheltered and appropriately dressed. Is Annabella an alcoholic?

Tito's Story

Tito, a thirty-six-year-old construction worker, had been married eleven years and had a ten-year-old son named Boris. He was a quiet man of few words who worked hard. Every week he gave his paycheck to his wife, Jeanine, who deposited it into their joint bank account.

Every day Tito came home directly from work, took care of a few chores, showered and then sat down to dinner with his wife and son. Jeanine always presented a lovely home-cooked meal including meat, potatoes and vegetables fresh from their garden. At each dinner Tito enjoyed two small glasses of homemade wine. His wine with dinner never made him drunk, but fatigue overcame him.

Tito worked hard by day, returned home to handle some chores, enjoyed his main meal with never more than two glasses of wine and then fell asleep on the living room couch for about an hour before finally getting ready for bed. Tito lived this routine day after day.

Catching his father between leaving the dinner table and arriving at the couch, Tito's son Boris asked him if he would shoot some hoops with him outside. Tito told Boris he was too tired and continued to the couch. His son walked away. Boris, like many boys his age, dreamed of becoming a professional basketball player—a dream that faded a little more on each occasion his father seemed not to have time for the boy nor have any interest in him.

Keith's Story

Keith, thirty-two years old, loved ice hockey. Two nights a week, often three, he went out with his friends to play hockey at the town arena. Afterwards he and the guys went to the local bar where they rehashed the game while pounding three, four or five brews.

One night, after hockey and drinks, Keith, considering himself sober, got into his truck to return home to his wife, Lara, and their three-month-old baby. This night Keith felt like having sex with his wife. He had always been attracted to his wife, even when she was looking somewhat disheveled while taking care of their little boy. Keith felt especially horny having had five beers and was looking forward to having sex with Lara. He couldn't wait to get home so he drove faster. But Keith didn't anticipate the DUI spot-check. He was pulled over by the police and was found to be in excess of the legal limit for blood alcohol content.

With his truck impounded and a hefty fine written on the ticket in his pocket but still feeling horny, Keith phoned Lara to pick him up.

Lara, having just managed a long nursing session with their son, which also hopefully cleared the blocked duct in her breast, felt fury overcome her at the thought of now having to disturb her sleeping baby in order to go out to pick up an even bigger baby. As Lara's car bounced along the road, the pain in her breast intensified and she was worried.

Lara arrived on the scene. Keith got in the car and as he leaned in to give his wife a kiss, he grabbed Lara's breast not even thinking it could be sore. Lara screamed and shoved Keith back causing him to hit his head on the side window. It was the kind of shove that took Lara as much off guard as it did Keith. Feeling insulted by the rebuff, Keith struck back with a slap across his wife's face. Seeming to emerge out of nowhere, the police who were manning the checkpoint hustled Keith from the car to the ground. He was handcuffed and taken to jail.

Maggie and Tom's Story

Maggie and Tom had been together for many years. They had three children: a boy, seventeen, and two girls, fourteen and ten. Although both had been steadily employed their whole adult lives, Maggie and Tom just made ends meet. Their friends considered them to be fun, responsible and sociable. They got along well and enjoyed life together.

Maggie and Tom admitted to being social drinkers. There was never any conflict between them about their alcohol use or anything else. They enjoyed a pint or two of beer together most nights on the back deck looking over the yard. They always drank in the company of friends. When they socialized they were apt to drink a little more, about four or five pints at a get-together.

Maggie and Tom were popular. Theirs was the home where the neighbors tended to congregate. Maggie and Tom socialized four to five times a week and considering the amount of alcoholic beverages they consumed on a friendly and sociable basis, they were each having twenty-four to thirty drinks every week. But there was never a foul word; never an argument.

Their eldest, seventeen-year-old Alan, also liked beer. He drank some eight to fifteen beers a week, usually with his parents (who believed that if he drank at home he would be safe). He was a good student, but given the family finances, his parents couldn't afford to send him to college. Alan was looking forward to working at a local garage where he hoped to become a mechanic someday. His teachers always felt he had the aptitude to become a mechanical engineer. A year later, Alan was involved in a car crash. The car rolled three times. Alan survived. His girlfriend, Lily, didn't.

Maggie and Tom's son was not intoxicated at the time of the car crash. But he had been the day before. No one blamed him. A deer had run across the road, causing Alan to veer suddenly. Police determined that Alan had been driving at an excessive speed, but he wasn't charged.

Alan's family toasted Lily's life at her wake. She was remembered as a lovely girl who aspired to work with children. Everyone mourned.

Brad's Story

Brad didn't think himself much of a drinker, because he only imbibed on occasion. Whereas his friends were out drinking every weekend, he drank, at the most, every other weekend, maybe twice a month. Brad was affable, funny and a good talker. When Brad did drink, he acted as though he was making up for lost time. He had eight to twelve drinks, getting drunk quickly and enjoying the buzz.

One day at the bar Brad found himself talking to Jessica, a girl sitting on the stool next to him. What Brad failed to notice was that the guy seated next to Jessica was getter angrier and angrier as Brad continued talking. Jessica was this other guy's girlfriend and he didn't like Brad spending so much time chatting with her. Suddenly the other guy stood up, walked around Jessica and grabbed Brad by the shirt collar. The guy punched Brad, who was knocked unconscious. When Brad woke up, he wasn't sure where he was or what had happened. His friends helped him from the bar to his car, where he slept it off.

Although Brad didn't drink as frequently as his friends did, the incident with the guy at the bar wasn't his only bad experience when intoxicated. There were several other occasions, including tripping over his own feet, puking at the wrong place and wrong time and blacking out.

ALCOHOL CONSUMPTION LEVELS

Before looking into what constitutes an alcoholic, let's first explore levels of alcohol consumption, discussed by Ernest L. Abel, Michael L. Kruger and John Friedl in "How Do Physicians Define 'Light,' 'Moderate,' and 'Heavy' Drinking?" in the journal *Alcoholism: Clinical and Experimental Research*. Alcohol consumption is divided into five categories: non-drinker, light, moderate, heavy and abusive. Determining the level of alcohol consumption is based upon standardized alcoholic units of measurement. One ounce of hard liquor equals four ounces of wine which equals one bottle of beer. The amount of alcohol in all three beverages is equivalent. What differs is the amount of water content. Even though some people want to believe that beer is less harmful than wine or that hard liquor is more harmful than the others, this is not really the case. What really matters is the amount of standardized units of alcohol consumed.

With respect to the amount of alcohol consumed as I discuss each level, it should be noted that these are the levels for men. The levels for women are determined to be about two-thirds that of men, according to the International Drinking Guidelines (http://www.icap .org/table/Internationaldrinkingguidelines).

Classification as a non-drinker doesn't automatically imply zero drinking of alcoholic beverages. A non-drinker may at times consume minor amounts of alcohol but never to such a degree so as to reach the criteria for being considered a light drinker. A non-drinker might have a drink at a special occasion, perhaps at a birthday, anniversary or New Year's Eve party. He or she will likely have only one alcoholic beverage. If he or she does have a second, this consumer will likely feel the effects of the alcohol and others are likely to take notice, if only to tease the consumer.

The next level of consumption is referred to as a light drinker. The light drinker consumes on average one to six standard alcoholic beverages weekly and not likely more than one to three per occasion. A person who consumes a glass of wine with dinner nightly is considered a light drinker as is a person who consumes three drinks an evening on each Friday and Saturday night.

Persons who consume on average twelve standard alcoholic beverages weekly are considered moderate drinkers. The consumption may dip down to half a dozen or up to maybe eighteen or so, but on average the moderate drinker consumes about a dozen beverages weekly and likely no more than three or four per occasion. A moderate drinker may have two alcoholic beverages with an evening meal or might consume three or four beverages per occasion three to four times a week or any pattern of consumption in between.

Heavy alcohol consumption is defined as, on average, twenty-four standard alcoholic beverages a week. Again, the numbers may dip down and may even exceed this quantity, but average out to twenty-four weekly. This person may consume a near-equal amount daily, say three beverages a day, or this person may consume greater quantities on particular days of the week totaling about twenty-four.

The term abusive in the context of alcohol consumption refers to the fact that consumption at this level and over the course of time can lead to physical ailments. Just like smoking cigarettes for years increases the likelihood of cancer and respiratory diseases, consuming alcohol at the abusive level increases the likelihood of alcohol-related illnesses. Common among these are diabetes, pancreatitis, esophageal cancer, cirrhosis of the liver and Korsakov's syndrome (a form of dementia most often seen in excessive consumers of alcohol); all awful ways to die and all preventable. Abusive drinking is consumption of thirty-five standard alcoholic beverages weekly on average. Regrettably, there are people who consume far in excess of thirty-five standard alcoholic beverages weekly with some remarkably abusive drinkers consuming double, triple and even quadruple that amount.

In addition to the five levels of alcohol consumption we've discussed, there is another category of consumption that isn't regarded as a level in the sense we've talked about, but rather refers to a pattern and minimal quantity of consumption: binge drinking. A binge drinker consumes five or more standard alcoholic beverages per occasion at least once per month. The goal of binge drinking is to consume enough alcohol so as to become intoxicated, to lose some degree of control of one's senses and feel the euphoria associated with that degree of intoxication. A binge drinker drinks with the express purpose of getting drunk, which poses risks. This person is at greater risk of unintentional injury and even death. This is the person who might trip on the way down the stairs and bash his or her head on the floor, resulting in anything from a bruise to a laceration to a permanent brain injury or death. The binge drinker is also more likely to be involved in violent altercations, even if he or she is not a violent person per se. This is the person who offends others, leading to physical retaliation. A binge drinker might also find him or herself unintentionally creating a child or, due to intoxication and lack of judgment at the time, getting into any kind of trouble.

Now let's return to the drinking habits of the men and women we've been discussing. In the first example, Annabella consumed at the rate of about one alcoholic beverage a day, putting her weekly average at about seven drinks. Given her rate of consumption, she meets the criteria for a light drinker. Although Tito's and Keith's patterns of consumption differ, their rates qualify them both as moderate drinkers, with Tito regularly consuming fourteen alcoholic beverages per week and Keith consuming anywhere between six and fifteen in any given week. As for Maggie and Tom, even though they consume at about the same rate, because of gender differences, Tom qualifies as a heavy drinker and Maggie as an abusive drinker. Brad, consuming at the rate of eight to twelve beverages per occasion at least once a month, meets criteria for being considered a binge drinker.

Notwithstanding the rate and level of consumption, the context of one's drinking habits also factor into the impact on oneself and others. There are substantial differences between drinkers in terms of the impact of their drinking on themselves and those around them. This leads us to a discussion of the definition of alcoholism.

ALCOHOLISM DEFINED

With regard to alcoholism, broadly speaking, there are actually two definitions. The first is a strictly medical definition and the second is psycho-social.

The medical definition of alcoholism rests on physiology and the concept of addiction. One is said to be addicted when one becomes physiologically dependent upon the substance. This means one's body has grown so accustomed to the substance that cessation of consumption leads to withdrawal symptoms. One needs the substance to function physiologically and without it, the body ceases to operate properly. If you are drinking at such a rate so as to create a physiological addiction such that cessation of consumption creates distress, you are also drinking at a rate to create other ailments as a result of ongoing consumption, according to the World Health Organization's "Lexicon of alcohol and drug terms."

Addiction becomes readily apparent when the consumer quickly and significantly reduces the rate of consumption or ceases consumption altogether. Just like one virus can create symptoms ranging from a cold to pneumonia in different people, levels of addiction can also range from light to moderate to severe and are best determined by the symptoms of withdrawal. Light withdrawal symptoms include headaches, fuzzy thinking and feeling poorly. Moderate symptoms include nausea, vomiting and alterations of mood. Severe symptoms can include depression, anxiety, delirium tremens and, in the most extreme cases, organ failure and death. Depending on how high alcohol consumption is and how severe the withdrawal, medical attention and supervision may be necessary to manage cessation. However, any degree of withdrawal symptoms indicates a substantial amount of alcohol consumption compromising physical health.

Although most people consider the medical definition of alcoholism when self-assessing alcohol abuse, this is not the definition used by most treating clinicians working with alcoholics. The more common definition from a clinical perspective is the psycho social one. This definition rests upon the impact of consumption from a psychological and social perspective. Factors considered from a psychological perspective include: feeling distressed about drinking; alterations of mood or personality; having tried to quit or reduce consumption only to find oneself consuming at the previous level again; forgetting about events when intoxicated (blackouts); sustaining accidental injuries; lying about, minimizing or concealing one's consumption; providing poor or lame excuses for consumption; projecting blame upon another for one's consumption.

Social factors considered include: upsetting another person (spouse, child, friend, employee/employer, client, stranger); interruption or alteration of work attendance; trouble with finances; not being able to meet an obligation; trouble with the law; complaints by others; violent behavior; being involved or potentially involved in a violent altercation; unplanned pregnancy; interruption or alteration of parenting capacity; being told one is an alcoholic by a loved one, friend, employer or healthcare professional.

Given the nature of the psycho-social definition of alcoholism, an alcoholic might not view him or herself as an alcoholic, yet someone affected by his or her drinking might. That a person doesn't consider him or herself to be an alcoholic doesn't mean that person is correct. It may be that the person's defense mechanisms, such as minimization, denial or blaming others, preclude the person from accurately or realistically self-assessing. Meeting criteria for a diagnosis of alcoholism does not hinge on belief or acceptance by the alcoholic but solely on such factors as noted. Strong self-defense mechanisms suggest that the person will have a more difficult time adjusting to the diagnosis and will likely be more resistant to treatment. This bodes poorly and it makes living with this person considerably more difficult and, in some cases, impossible.

RETURNING TO ANNABELLA

Annabella presents a complex case. While she doesn't drink much in relative terms, her drinking coincides with meeting the emergent needs of her children.

Consider her daughters. Serita may feel that no amount of success is ever good enough to warrant her mother's immediate praise. Will she grow up to be a perfectionist, wondering just how good she must be to attain her mother's approval or will she give up, feeling defeated and thinking, *What's the use*? Jocelyn might believe that no one can save her from being bullied. Will she grow up believing this is her lot in life? If she finds herself in an abusive relationship, will she be inclined to stay, assuming this is normal? Teresa likely feels her mother doesn't care for her. How hysterical must Teresa become in order to have her needs met?

Annabella is probably depressed and, although she loves her daughters, her girls also represent a deviation from the vocation and life she thought she would have. Choosing alcohol only worsens her problems. Alcohol is a depressant and consumption causes a person like Annabella to feel worse. When compounded with the realization that she is not available to meet the emotional needs of her children— the result of choosing to drink just when her children need her—she feels worse still. From a psycho-social perspective, Annabella meets the criteria for being considered alcoholic, even though severity and driving factors are open for discussion.

TITO'S DIAGNOSIS

Tito, although likely a good and responsible person, is unavailable for his son. His son isn't looking for much from his dad, just a little time to play basketball and to feel special in the eyes of his father. All Tito is doing is falling asleep on the couch after work, following chores and dinner. But what if Tito, instead of two glasses of wine a night, only had one? Might he feel less fatigued and might he be able to meet the needs of his son? At fourteen beverages weekly and with the impact on his relationship with his son, Tito meets the criteria for being considered alcoholic. If Tito were able to be there for his son or if Tito reduced his consumption to enable his availability, then he wouldn't meet the criteria even though consuming at a light level, similar to Annabella. Interestingly, it is not just quantity of consumption that determines meeting the criteria for alcoholism but also context.

KEITH'S ALCOHOLISM

Keith's defense mechanism causes him to deny he is too drunk to drive and his level of intoxication alters his personality, contributing to a heightened sexual desire. His consumption leads to a run-in with the law, an upset spouse, physical altercations and distress in his marriage. Keith meets the criteria for being considered alcoholic. He is using and abusing.

The level of distress he creates extends beyond himself to his wife, child and community by virtue of police involvement. On this night he receives a major wake-up call. He is at risk of losing his license and being charged with sexual assault for grabbing his wife's breast and also with physical assault for slapping her. Although he and others may claim she shoved him, remember this was after he grabbed her breast and only in self-defense. Keith is alcoholic and is in deep trouble on an individual level, not to mention his trouble with his family and marriage.

MAGGIE AND TOM'S IMPLICATIONS

Maggie and Tom appear to be law-abiding citizens and respectable neighbors who are raising a good family. It appears superficially that all is well. Deeper scrutiny reveals a host of concerns.

Maggie's and Tom's levels of consumption have normalized alcohol use for their children. For children who grow up in families where there is alcohol consumption, what they witness becomes their normal. What they witness can become not the limit of their own consumption during adolescence and adulthood but rather the starting point. Maggie and Tom's son, Alan, is already consuming at a moderate rate at seventeen years of age. He is under the legal drinking age, even though some jurisdictions do permit under-age drinking in the home of the parent with alcohol provided by a parent. However, Maggie's and Tom's levels of consumption and permissive attitudes toward their son's underage drinking create in their son an attitude of defiance; he can break social rules and get away with it. This leads to an increased likelihood of risk-taking behavior, exemplified by his driving at excessive speeds, being intoxicated the day before the crash and likely driving while fatigued although perhaps not realizing it.

A case of beer costs about forty dollars in Canada and about twenty-five dollars in the United States. Between Maggie and Tom, not to mention their son, they spend three hundred twenty dollars a month in Canada or two hundred dollars a month in the United States on beer. Over the course of fifteen years that amounts to $57,600 in Canada and $36,000 in the United States. The amount of money spent on beer by Maggie and Tom, if saved for their son's education instead, would result in not only a boy less likely to consume alcohol at a high rate, but also potentially enough money, with interest, to pay for the cost of a college education.

Although their son was intellectually capable, Alan's drinking coincided with a lack of financial planning to create the conditions that prevented him from attending college and bettering himself through education.

If Maggie and Tom didn't normalize a high level of alcohol consumption for their children, Alan's girlfriend might still be alive and Maggie wouldn't be at risk for alcohol-related diseases, due to her consuming alcohol at an abusive level. Here is a situation where no one feels any particular distress from alcohol consumption, yet the implications are staggering, including death. Just because one does not perceive a problem doesn't mean there isn't one.

BRAD'S DIAGNOSIS

Brad meets the criteria for being considered an alcoholic. He drinks to excess on a more than monthly basis. He suffers blackouts and unintended injuries and has found himself in physical altercations not of his choosing. Brad is a heavy binge drinker.

RECOVERY STAGES

Working with alcoholics can be challenging. Just getting an alcoholic to admit his or her alcoholism can be a daunting task. In terms of recovery, five stages are identified: pre-contemplation, contemplation, preparation, action and maintenance.

In the pre-contemplation stage of recovery, either the affected person hasn't yet been identified with alcoholism or the person has been told but is in abject denial. There is no reasoning with this person; he or she is not ready to address the problem of alcoholism. Pursuing the issue with a person in the pre-contemplation stage may lead to an escalation of conflict. Persons living with or affected by this person may come to feel they are the ones with the problem. At times these people are more affected than the person who may seem to get by through living in denial.

During the contemplation stage the affected person considers the notion of alcoholism. He or she is just coming to recognize that alcohol consumption could be an issue and this person struggles with the realization. While not denying being an alcoholic, this person may still minimize the extent of the problem and/or project blame onto others for problems originating with him or herself. The good news is that this person is coming to appreciate that he or she has a problem to some degree.

In the preparation stage, the person has come to terms with the notion of being considered alcoholic and ponders doing something about it. What to do can be a struggle and the thought of any intervention may require considerable deliberation by the affected person.

As the affected person resolves that action must be taken, the next stage of recovery is implementing the plan of action. Here the person forthrightly seeks to limit, reduce or cease consumption of alcohol as determined by a plan. The person also attends necessary treatments and receives physical and mental health care as necessary.

Assuming a successful implementation of the action plan, the person has to contend with relapse prevention or maintenance of sobriety. This is achieved by addressing issues that may have previously contributed to conditions leading to alcohol consumption and by putting support mechanisms in place, such as attendance at group meetings for recovering alcoholics. The benefit of a maintenance plan is that it respects the fact that recovery and sobriety are issues that the alcoholic might face daily or at times of greater stress and upheaval over the course of a lifetime.

Rarely do people progress through the five stages of recovery neatly. More often there is a tug and pull between the various stages. There are two steps forward with one step back or, at times, a full slide back to the very beginning. This makes living with an alcoholic difficult, tumultuous, confusing, upsetting, but, it is hoped, one day rewarding.

PARTNER/SPOUSE CHALLENGES

In addition to there being challenges for the recovering alcoholic, there are also challenges for the partner or spouse of the alcoholic. He or she may get into heated debates with the alcoholic about the extent of alcohol use and its impact on the affected person and relationship. The partner might, at times, think him or herself crazy, believe him or herself responsible for the affected person's alcohol use and be embarrassed or intimidated by the alcoholic's alterations of personality or aggressive or dangerous behavior as a result of alcohol use. These issues can alter or interfere with the ability of the partner or spouse to manage matters, handle finances and keep him or herself and the children safe.

There might be a tendency for the partner to minimize or even deny the issue of alcoholism or to live life so as not to upset the alcoholic. When a partner is affected in such a way, then this person inadvertently contributes to a set of conditions that facilitate the ongoing issues. The partner becomes an enabler: someone whose behavior directly or indirectly facilitates the ongoing consumption of alcohol and alcoholism. The partner is not to blame for the affected person's consumption, but he or she isn't making matters any better and contributes to the perpetuation of the problem. For these reasons, partners and other affected family members (children, siblings, parents) need treatment and support in their own right to learn about their roles as enablers, how to cope more effectively and how to resist engaging in behaviors that might otherwise prolong the problems from which they seek relief.

WITHDRAWAL AND REHABILITATION

Depending on the degree of addiction, a function of the quantity of alcohol consumed, various interventions, treatments and intensity of help should be considered. If one is a heavy drinker, there is a likelihood of withdrawal symptoms ranging from mild to moderate. These withdrawal symptoms probably won't require hospitalization, but they might be eased with some medical intervention and a good diet. If one is an abusive drinker, there is a likelihood that hospitalization might be required to manage more serious physical symptoms of withdrawal. For abusive drinkers it is always better if withdrawal is medically supervised. Hospitalization to manage withdrawal symptoms is generally from three to five days in duration.

Managing withdrawal symptoms is separate from managing sobriety. Heavy and abusive drinkers might need considerable support to resist consuming alcohol in the initial stages of cessation. These persons might require a stay at an inpatient rehabilitation facility, remaining in care anywhere from a week to several months, depending on the severity of their desire and physical cravings as a result of addiction.

Light and moderate drinkers are less likely to suffer physical withdrawal symptoms but still will have difficulty resisting the urge to drink, particularly in the initial stages of recovery. To support the recovery of the light and moderate drinker, outpatient support groups offer places to meet and gain support to strengthen one's resolve and ability to resist temptation. Outpatient support groups are also strongly recommended for persons exiting inpatient treatment.

SUPPORT GROUPS

The most well-researched group program to support sobriety is Alcoholics Anonymous (AA). Known for its 12-step program, AA offers support groups in nearly every community throughout North America and most countries throughout the world. AA groups are also available at many popular holiday destinations and even on cruise ships, making AA a portable system of support that helps people with recovery and the maintenance of sobriety by allowing them to work through the 12 steps almost any place, almost any time. Not attending AA is working against oneself, although people come up with many excuses to avoid what AA offers. Those excuses include not being alcoholic "enough," not believing in a higher spiritual power, not believing one is fully responsible for oneself and believing that cessation of consumption equals recovery. It doesn't matter what the excuse; if you reach the criteria for being considered alcoholic, then AA can be beneficial for you.

Stopping consumption does not mean recovery. Associated with consumption is distorted thinking—the lies you have learned to tell yourself about your life that contributed to consumption and relationship challenges. Quitting drinking doesn't mean that the associated thinking has gone away. In attending AA, over time you will come to understand the conditions that led to your abuse of alcohol and the impact of your drinking on your well-being as well as the well-being of others, including partners, spouses, children, siblings, parents, relatives, friends, colleagues and clients. Eventually you will come to understand the cognitive distortions created in your mind that contributed to your problematic consumption of alcohol and associated relationship difficulties.

Not only for adult alcoholics, Alcoholics Anonymous has branched out to the development of Alateen and Al-Anon, groups providing support service for teenagers and family affected by an alcoholic family member. Alateen and Al-Anon help family members affected by an alcoholic parent, spouse, sibling or child to differentiate their responsibility from that of the affected person. These groups also help family members cope and better manage the impact from the behavior of the alcoholic. They help the attendees reorganize their own thinking that is so often distorted by the alcoholic. Such groups are vital for children who may feel responsible for the well-being of the alcoholic or the other parent and for spouses who themselves may have been affected by the upset and turmoil created by the alcoholic.

In addition to group support services, couples or marital therapy is necessary to repair the damage brought on by alcoholism. This therapy is directed toward facilitating improved communication and coping strategies between the spouses so they may handle life's tribulations more effectively without having to resort to maladaptive strategies such as alcohol consumption. This therapy is also to provide information about alcohol, alcoholism and other treatment services as may be necessary and to provide a place for the couple to explore their backgrounds and relationship.

Therapy can also help the couple understand and support their children more effectively through the recovery stages and mainte-nance of sobriety.

Many affected persons and sometimes their partners wonder if the affected person can ever drink again. They may wonder if they can attend functions where alcohol is available and they may wonder whether the other partner must cease to consume. All these issues and more can and should be addressed in the context of couples ther-apy. If there is a concern, it should be raised and, to whatever degree possible, resolved.

CONTROLLING OR CEASING CONSUMPTION

Whether or not a person has to cease consumption altogether depends on a number of variables. Chief among those variables is the pattern of drinking for the consumer. Does one drink lead to two and do two lead to three and so on? For many alcoholics, there is no such thing as just one drink. These persons are not good candidates for controlled drinking. Another indicator of concern is alteration of personality. If the consumption of alcohol leads to a person acting differently, becoming more aggressive, promiscuous or jovial for example, then controlled drinking may also be contraindicated. If the recovering alcoholic is prone to depression or currently taking medications incompatible with alcohol, then controlled drinking is also inappro-priate. Fighting for controlled drinking and not being willing to stop completely are indicators that one's lust for alcohol will likely inter-fere with other, more pressing priorities and suggests that the person should not be drinking at all.

In view of one's alcohol consumption and looking at one's mar-riage, one's partner might be upset, intimidated, concerned or wor-ried about one's consumption. Even one drink may cause distress to one's significant other. If the partner has a history with an alcoholic parent, then a person's drinking may trigger anxiety in that partner. If one accepts that a marriage is more important than alcohol, then one shouldn't drink. A person who seeks to negotiate this with his or her partner is implying that the craving for alcohol trumps the sense of safety and security the person can provide for his or her partner by quitting fully and forever. While a person may win the battle allowing him or her still to consume, the person will have lost a fulfilling relationship. A person must choose what is more important: alcohol or one's spouse.

ILLICIT DRUGS

What about illicit drugs such as marijuana, ecstasy, cocaine, heroin, amphetamines, barbiturates or prescription drugs like codeine or oxycodone?

Risk factors to relationships including any of these substances parallel those of alcoholism, but there are some important differences. Depending on the substance, there are different impacts from a psychological perspective as well as in terms of personality disposition.

Johnny and Eileen's Story

Johnny always thought of himself as cool and easygoing. That is what attracted his wife, Eileen, to him. Eileen's father was hotheaded. She didn't want to marry a man like her father and when she met Johnny at a concert, she felt he was very different. As the concert started, Johnny lit up a joint. He took a long toke, blew the smoke past Eileen and then, without reservation, passed the joint forward for her to take a hit. Eileen wasn't much of a pot smoker, but she couldn't resist feeling cool and somewhat rebellious. Smoking pot provided by an attractive guy at an open-air stadium concert seemed to fit her at the time. Needless to say, a relationship developed.

Johnny and Eileen married and had two children, both girls. Eileen worked hard to make their finances meet their needs and Johnny, ever so easygoing, did only what he needed to get by. Even at home, Eileen seemed to take on the major share of the household work while Johnny mellowed.

One day, worried about finances, Eileen suggested to Johnny that he apply for the supervisor's position just offered at his company. Johnny said he would think about it, but he never followed through. After some months, Eileen broached the issue of concern underlying her suggestion to Johnny that he consider the supervisor's position. She told him she was tired of working so hard, was worried about money and wanted him to get a better-paying job.

Johnny thought about Eileen's upset and request. Then he came up with a plan of his own. Rather than just grow a little marijuana to support his personal use, he would cultivate extra plants to sell among his friends. He shared his plan with Eileen, who was outraged.

But Johnny didn't see anything wrong. He had been smoking pot for so many years that not much mattered to him anymore. What appeared as an ability to take things in stride had turned into something more sinister, the outcome of chronic pot use. But neither Johnny nor Eileen realized it at the time.

HEALTH HAZARDS

Although many persons consider marijuana to be an innocuous substance, this is far from the truth. While occasional use may not create any disturbance on an individual basis, chronic or habitual use very often leads to amotivational syndrome or what I like to call "lack of gumption." This refers to a sense of apathy resulting in difficulty attending to task completion. Afflicted people find it difficult to get things done while either intoxicated by marijuana or affected by chronic usage. Students might have falling or failing grades from chronic use. Spouses might let household responsibilities go unmet or poorly achieved. Parents might become inadvertently permissive, not taking enough care to hold a child accountable to reasonable

expectations or outright neglect. If usage alters personality, it is usually in the direction of making someone more mellow—consistent
with lying on the couch frequently. The problem this imposes comes
when one's responsibilities are not met to the satisfaction of another
or a person is placed at risk of harm due to the user's inattention.

Beyond these individual and social problems, chronic marijuana
use creates health hazards similar to smoking cigarettes. Marijuana
users take carcinogenic substances very deep into their lungs and
over time it increases their risk of cancer and respiratory diseases.
As if these impacts of marijuana use weren't bad enough, it is still an
illicit substance in most jurisdictions. Possession of any appreciable
quantity, sharing/selling among friends and distributing for or without profit are all illegal activities that can bring a person into conflict
with the law. A conviction for a drug-related offense, even "only marijuana," can undermine current employment, future employability
and the ability to cross international borders.

For those who seek to distort the issue in their favor by citing
the medical use of marijuana, chronic personal use for recreational
purposes is vastly different from medical use. With medical use, the
use of the substance is weighed against the benefit derived in relationship to the hardship imposed by the illness. Only after a cost/
benefit analysis in terms of the relief provided weighed against the
distress of a particular disease is marijuana prescribed. Even if prescribed, the physical and psychological side effects remain but are
accepted as the price of coping better with the disease, typically one
which is degenerative in nature.

An otherwise healthy person may feel relaxed or experience
some degree of euphoria when smoking marijuana, but typically the
side effects outweigh the gain, especially in the context of a relationship where the other partner may be worried about the legal implications of possession, selling or use, the impact on gumption and ability
to meet responsibilities and the effect on health.

As with marijuana use, similar health and social concerns hold
true for other illicit substances. Of greater concern with other illicit

substances are the higher risks of forming an addiction and serious alterations of personality (e.g., paranoia, hysteria, narcissism). Along with these greater concerns are the increased likelihood of relationship conflicts and the challenges of supporting oneself vocationally with any degree of stability. Sadly, even prescription drugs such as heavy-duty pain killers can lead to similar concerns.

TREATMENT OPTIONS

Like the alcoholic, if you or your loved one are encumbered by a drug habit or addiction, then treatment will be necessary to abstain and maintain abstinence. Depending on the drug and the severity of addiction, you may require detoxification with a short hospital stay, ongoing medical supervision (e.g., methadone treatment) and long-term support similar to Alcoholics Anonymous. In the context of substance abuse and addiction, the group support program Narcotics Anonymous (NA) is modeled on the AA program. Though it is less accessible in rural areas, it is usually available in most urban settings.

As easygoing a guy as Johnny was, his chronic drug use and so-called mellow disposition worked against his gaining help. He had no ambition for giving up his drug of choice. Not that he felt strongly; in fact he didn't feel much of anything and so couldn't muster the motivation for change. He presented himself as happy just the way he was. He conveyed a passive form of resistance to Eileen, who decided she couldn't continue to live with him. Eileen worried that Johnny's marijuana crops would be discovered by the police at some point and that their daughters would be influenced by his habit and unlawful activity.

When Eileen left Johnny, it was to return home for support. Her father, although he had a bad temper, wasn't lazy or drug addicted and readily accepted Eileen and the children into his home. Eileen didn't worry about any legal action to maintain care and control of the children. She knew that Johnny wouldn't get around to doing anything about it.

DECISION TIME

If you are using drugs in a way that contributes to any kind of distress, either for yourself or for a loved one, then stop and get help. Prioritize your well-being and that of your relationship over the substance. If you are the partner of someone using, someone unable to help him or herself or make use of available supports, get help. Learn to differentiate your partner's issues from your own and take care of yourself before losing yourself along with the user.

The Winner's Motto:
I am fully present in my relationship
with body, mind and spirit.

Using Violence in Any Form

The Sinner's Motto: I win.

I want this; you want that. I do things this way; you do things another way. Differences are inevitable, but in some relationships differences, big and small, lead to physical or verbal conflict. Conflict occurs when differences cannot be resolved reasonably and to everyone's satisfaction and where the resolution process or outcome creates distress.

The ability to resolve differences in advance of them becoming conflicts and to settle conflicts in a way that leaves people feeling reasonable about the issue depend on emotional maturity, creative thinking, flexibility, disposition to fairness and the ability to take a long term perspective on life. However, if you are the kind of person who quickly gets caught up in the immediacy of the moment, flusters or angers easily and believes that your needs have to come first, then marriage can become a battleground.

Nadia and Phillip's Story

Nadia could turn a sarcastic phrase faster than anyone. Cross her or displease her and she attacked you verbally. Nadia took offense easily, so it was difficult not to cross her. Her sarcastic quips were always delivered with a smirk. Because she delivered her comments with jest, if anyone ever took offense, she used her trustworthy excuses: "I'm just kidding," "I'm just being funny," "Can't you take a joke?" or her favorite, "Don't be so sensitive."

When they first dated, her husband Phillip thought Nadia was funny and really smart to have such a quick wit. However, now that he and the children were the brunt of her barbs, he was not amused. Phillip felt that Nadia's comments were hurtful and that the children had become meanspirited and verbally vicious between themselves as a result of Nadia's model of behavior.

One day a school administrator phoned Phillip and Nadia about their ten-year-old daughter, Calley. She had been posting nasty comments about another girl, who apparently did nothing to Calley to provoke the attack, on her blog, creating drama among all the girls in the class.

On the way to meet with the principal, Nadia told her husband that she would do the talking. At the beginning of the meeting, Nadia took an aggressive position. She suggested to the principal that her daughter must have just cause to make derogatory comments about the other girl. Phillip bit his lip. The principal made the school's position very clear: Calley's behavior was considered bullying and she expected Calley to remove the offensive comments and apologize to her classmate.

Nadia wouldn't back down. She took the view that it was her daughter who was being persecuted. There was no resolution to the problem.

The next day Calley's teacher, in an effort to restore peace in the classroom, seated Nadia's daughter on the other side of the room from the girl whom she offended. This added to Nadia's sense that her daughter was being persecuted unjustly. Nadia's daughter fueled the sentiment and complained daily about the poor treatment she received from her teacher.

Believing they were fighting a losing battle, Nadia felt that she should change her daughter's school to alleviate the situation and give her daughter a fresh start. In reality, she was avoiding taking responsibility for deploying a strategy that not only backfired, but also reinforced the bullying behavior of her daughter.

Nadia's husband Phillip was reluctant to confront her. Phillip didn't like being the brunt of her sarcasm and he knew she was able to spit out nasty comments faster than he was able to defend himself. Since he couldn't communicate with Nadia and get their conversation direction on the right track, he chose to spend more time at work. Nadia continued to manage the children and their choice of schools.

VERBAL ABUSE

Who is more sensitive when one partner accuses another of verbal abuse? Very often it is the person who is verbally abusive who is actually the more sensitive one. This person is using verbal abuse as a means to defend him or herself from feelings of inadequacy. Although sarcasm can appear funny, it is rarely a laughing matter. Sarcasm is best understood as verbal abuse disguised as humor. Upon confrontation, because the delivery is made with humor, the deliverer can defend him or herself just as Nadia did. This leaves the target of the message questioning him or herself, because the abuser's defense mechanism obscures the situation just enough to take the blame off the deliverer. Too often the sarcastic individual is funny as well as hurtful and is so quick witted that those who would confront him or her are no match. This means that these situations can go on seemingly forever. Verbal abuse hurts tremendously, undermines self-esteem and creates depression and anxiety in the target. Because there are no physical bruises, the abuser continues with a sense of impunity.

The quality of your partnership, the impact on your family and the behavior of your children can be greatly affected by sarcasm. Sarcasm as verbal abuse and a form of bullying is cancerous to a relationship. Although it might appear to create the conditions allowing one to dismiss responsibilities or take advantage of others, from a social perspective it injures people's spirits and makes for lopsided relationships where one may achieve a goal but at the expense of another person. Sarcasm is not funny to the one who is the brunt of the humor-disguised verbal assault. If you use sarcasm and if you think you are keeping, maintaining or bettering a relationship by it, look more closely. That your partner, the target of your brand of humor, is not complaining might merely be indicative of him or her being under-powered to defend against you.

Take a very close look at your relationships and you are likely to see people who say things only to placate you, all the while either distancing themselves from you or aligning with you to avoid being the brunt of your criticisms. In other words, your partner, family members and friends either stay away or tell you what you want to hear so they won't have to be subject to your acerbic tongue. If you were given this book by your partner, it might be because you exhibit this behavior and your partner is hoping that if you read about your problem, you might finally understand and change your ways.

If you use sarcasm and are verbally abusive, you need to stop projecting your sensitivity onto others and take responsibility for being abusive. Tell your partner that you are sensitive, if that is the issue, or tell your partner you hate to lose, if that is the issue. If you don't know what the issue is but now realize you are sarcastic and verbally abusive, apologize and seek to change your behavior. Taking responsibility for the behavior in yourself will then give you the moral authority to address similar behavior in your children. I assume you want your children to grow up to be liked and admired, to have friends with whom they can speak freely and discuss matters in such a way as to leave everyone feeling good about each other. I imagine you don't want your partner to feel beaten up and seek to avoid or placate you just to elude your bitter speech. Desist in the sarcastic behavior. Seek counseling to learn what motivates your negative behavior so that the behavior may become unnecessary and so that you can have a mutually-fulfilling marriage.

TAKING RESPONSIBILITY FOR SARCASM

Whereas sarcasm is all about pointing the finger at someone else, recovery is all about taking personal responsibility and changing abusive behavior. Think about what you want to say right now. If you have a quick quip ready to fire at me, the author, that's the best evidence that you are still defensive about your problem and offensive in your management. That is the tip-off that you need help and counseling. Assuming you love your partner and children, if you have them, then stop the sarcasm, think about the impact of what you want to say and learn to talk about your issues.

If you are the victim of a sarcastic partner and you find you cannot escape his or her vicious wit, tell your partner. Explain that you are hurt when humor is used to deliver upsetting comments and put-downs. Add that the fact that you do not have quick retorts to your partner's quips doesn't make his or her sarcastic behavior right. Tell your partner that due to his or her behavior you have learned not to speak your mind and that you feel sad about the loss of emotional intimacy in the relationship as a result. Let your partner know you love him or her and wish that things could be different. Ask your partner if the two of you could talk about this more sincerely, with or without the help of a counselor, because you don't want this to interfere in your relationship any longer. Then, and likely to the surprise of your partner, apologize for not letting him or her know sooner in your relationship or know more meaningfully and honestly how you

were feeling and how you behaved differently as a result. Hopefully
that will open up a dialogue that can lead to change.

Sometimes, though, the issues are more sinister than sarcasm.
For some, life can be downright dangerous and nasty.

Derek and Joanne's Story

By the time Derek was a teenager, he considered his dad an asshole and
his mother a wimp. He learned that if he wanted anything, he had to get it
himself and if he wanted to keep anything, he had to fight to hang onto it.
Derek's attitude got him in trouble, though he managed to avoid serious altercations with the law. Conflict at school eventually got him expelled even
though he claimed leaving was his choice.

Derek left home at seventeen after a vicious fight with his father. It happened just as his dad was going to hit his mother again. He beat up his dad.

Derek was industrious and got a job as a welder. He enjoyed the fruits of his
labor. Derek parlayed his welding skills and what he had learned watching
the owner of the shop where he worked into his own business by the time
he was twenty-three. He "acquired" some of his former boss's accounts and
this gave him the start he needed to work for himself.

By the time Derek was twenty-eight, he had managed to secure enough
contracts that he ran the business and hired others to do the labor. Derek
took tremendous pride in his accomplishments and considered himself a
self-made man. He drove a nice car and lived in a small but luxurious house.

Derek had filtered through a number of relationships by the time he met
Joanne. She was twenty-six and was quickly taken in by Derek's accomplishments, looks and charm. She was smitten with Derek and loved his
ability to know what he wanted and go after it. She felt adored when he
told her which of her clothes she looked best in, ultimately deciding her
wardrobe, and she felt pampered and spoiled when he ordered for her
in the fanciest restaurants, even if his picks weren't her first choice. His

choices were more expensive, so she felt she could hardly say no and risk insulting him.

After meeting Joanne's friends, Derek decided that they were better off in each other's exclusive company. He got moody and snippy with Joanne at the mere suggestion that they go out with another couple or she visit with her girlfriends. He thought they should be available just to each other and anything or anyone that got in the way was just an irritant to their perfect relationship. After all, with his money they had everything they could want.

Derek proposed marriage in a lavish restaurant. At the end of the meal he rose from his seat to proclaim his love for Joanne. He withdrew a diamond ring from his pocket and asked the question. Joanne felt flushed with emotion. She accepted his proposal. The restaurant patrons rose and applauded. A video appeared on the Internet within minutes. It was Derek's crowning achievement.

Derek and Joanne had a small wedding, just the two of them, on the beach in a tropical paradise. Their vacation was their honeymoon. When they returned, Joanne moved into Derek's home and that's where things started to fall apart.

Joanne's belongings took more space in the closet than allotted by Derek. His garments were pressed tightly to accommodate. When he saw creases in his clothes, he became angry. He admonished Joanne for her insensitivity to his wardrobe and advised that he felt personally disrespected by her causing creases in his garments, garments he was to wear to impress clients when hoping to close contracts. He felt that her insensitivity jeopardized his business and financial security. He couldn't understand how she could be so thoughtless. Joanne was devastated.

Given the ferocity of Derek's tirade and in view of his prior generosity and attention, Joanne felt she must have truly transgressed to give rise to such an angry reaction. She felt she had truly hurt his feelings and was deeply ashamed. She apologized and promised to be more respectful of his space and things. With that Derek thought he may have overreacted and he made a half-hearted apology that was limited in scope by the defense that he only acted the way he did because he was feeling hurt by Joanne's disrespect in view of all he did for her. That he gave an apology at all, even a defensive one, helped Joanne accept the intensity of his tirade.

As time passed, Joanne learned that Derek had a number of rules he expected her to follow. He insisted and she agreed to leave her job to stay at home to take care of him. With few friends left, no job and rigid rules to follow, Joanne's life shrunk to attending to Derek's needs.

Derek criticized Joanne for her housekeeping, believing she could do a better job with the time available. Joanne grew miserable. A home and situation that had looked like paradise was beginning to seem a lot more like a prison. Joanne's libido began to diminish and Derek became increasingly demanding. Soon she discovered he was an avid porn viewer and was of the opinion that, as a couple, they should play out what he saw in the adult videos.

As Joanne's sex drive continued to diminish, Derek became even more demanding, seeking to live out his sexual fantasies. From time to time Joanne obliged minor fantasies, thinking this would pacify him. She became good at pretending to enjoy herself only to feel more ashamed of how she was being used. Derek was oblivious to Joanne's feelings and thought himself a lucky man to have such an obliging wife whom he believed was a willing and active participant in his sexual desires.

One day Derek made a demand which Joanne would not oblige. She was disgusted by the suggestion and slapped Derek's face. Feeling more disrespected than he ever did before and feeling a rage that had been building since before his altercation with his father, the aftermath of which caused him to leave home, he swung at Joanne. With one hit he blackened her eye and bloodied her nose.

Joanne had no place to go, nowhere to run, no family to save her, no friends to intervene. She had no money and being out of the workplace left her with limited employment opportunities. Joanne was trapped. With blood on her face she acquiesced and met Derek's sexual demands. Her shame locked her in. She was now totally his.

Derek gave her flowers the next day and an apology that was all too familiar. It was the kind of apology that blamed the victim, excusing the behavior of the perpetrator: "I'm sorry for what I did, but it was only because of what you had done." This was now Joanne's lot in life.

Joanne learned not to press back, not to challenge, just to be meek. Derek had inadvertently recreated the roles of his birth family. He was an asshole and Joanne a wimp.

RESOLVING CONFLICT

Resolving conflict requires people to acknowledge the needs and wants of others and to manage the intensity of their own emotions. It requires a disposition that you won't always get your own way and that there are more important things than winning. Resolving conflict requires the maturity to recognize that there may be more than one way, more than your way, to get things done.

Derek was raised believing that "might is right" and that if you earn it, it is yours alone. He grew up learning that men come first and that those around you are there to serve your needs ahead of their own. Derek, although seeking to leave the environment in which he was steeped, knew little else himself. Like his father, Derek was coercive, controlling and intimidating. In her own right Joanne, for whatever reasons, was naive, needy, blind or just a hapless bystander.

As their relationship progressed, Derek controlled Joanne's dress, space, friends, family, money, vocation, housing and body. His strategies included psychological manipulation, direct demands, guilt, shame, blame, physical violence and sexual assault. He limited Joanne's world, stripped her of relationships, cut off her access to resources beyond his own and squashed her dignity and self-worth. Some might say he hit her only once and seek to limit the extent to which people like Derek are perceived as violent. However, violent behavior is defined beyond just physical terms. All of Derek's behaviors meet the criteria for violence, just of differing types.

Derek was financially, emotionally, psychologically and socially violent as well as physically and sexually violent. That he hit Joanne just once only suggests that that was all it took to intimidate Joanne and drive her into submission. If she hadn't been subdued by that one act, more physical violence would have followed until the objective of domination was complete. "Only one hit" is the refrain of the abuser or the victim trying to dismiss or minimize the violence and the intent of the violence—intimidation and coercion to meet one's needs ahead of, or to the exclusion of, another's. One hit doesn't mean that is all that would occur; it means that was all that was necessary to dominate and so the physical violence appeared to cease. Knowing what could happen, Joanne learned to never again press her needs, contradict her husband or reject his bidding. Derek didn't need to hit her any more. His job was done.

There is little likelihood of a relationship like Derek's and Joanne's improving on its own. The extent of Derek's tyranny is unknown. How far he will go to continue to dominate and control hasn't been tested. In circumstances like these, victims learn not to push as their lives might be at stake. Some who have tested the extent of their partners' tyrannies have been permanently injured and died. This is a dangerous situation. Relationships such as this may be subject to change as a result of crisis. The crisis may include hospitalization of the abused, police intervention, criminal charges against the perpetrator and threat of divorce.

SAFETY FIRST

If the abused contemplates change by any circumstance, safety should be the first and highest priority before initiating change. When the abuser feels challenged by the abused seeking change, there is a heightened risk for the escalation of violence. The abuser may feel even more disrespected by the audacity of the abused to seek to leave or change the status of the relationship. The abuser may genuinely feel a heartfelt need to hold the relationship together but only has violent behavior on which to rely to address his or her feelings and achieve his or her goal.

Intensification of the violence remains a potential outcome and therefore steps must be contemplated and carried out to keep people safe from harm during the implementation and process of change. For women this means putting in place a safety plan, as women are disproportionately likely to be the targets of such violence and are more likely to be injured or die at the hands of this kind of violent partner than men.

A safety plan includes considering and then planning for all the things needed to take care of oneself and any children prior to implementing change. Consider what is necessary to manage on one's own, without the support of the partner. Plan for a place to stay, have financial resources and acquire transportation as well as important documents such as passport, driver's license, insurance certificates and diplomas. Also include access to electronic records, passwords and data.

A safety plan must take into account the possibility of violent action on the part of the abuser and include strategies to keep the abused safe from threats, intimidation or direct physical violence. Many larger communities have shelters for abused women. Women who are contemplating a change in a violent/abusive relationship are advised to seek guidance and support from women's shelters. The staff are well trained and experienced in helping women who are subject to abuse. Seeking guidance does not mean one needs or is seeking shelter. However, if shelter is an advisable component of a safety plan, by first attending counseling at the shelter a woman can be apprised of the shelter's location and resources. Many shelters, apart from providing safe residence, also provide legal and other forms of social support. Many include space for children and enable the children to maintain their studies. Safety should be the primary consideration for the abused, whether seeking to improve or to leave the relationship.

THE VIOLENT PARTNER

If you are the violent/abusive partner and you want to mend your ways and sincerely want to maintain your relationship, not just in your own interest but also in that of your partner, then seek help for yourself. Take responsibility and acknowledge your anger and violent behavior—all of it. You need to see past your physically and/or sexually aggressive behavior to include the psychological, emotional and other forms of abuse, such as limiting access to financial or social resources. You must seek help to address the source of your anger and learn anger management strategies as well as how to cope with stress. You should also learn about your attitude toward gender differences and, where necessary, about the impact of your formative experiences in your family of origin on your point of view.

Throughout your process of self-discovery, you need to realize that even if it's your objective to improve your relationship such that it may continue, this may not be your partner's objective. If you have different goals with respect to the relationship, you will have to come to terms with this and realize that your partner has the right to leave you. Wanting to maintain the relationship does not mean it will continue. Your ability to accept this peacefully will be evidence that treatment is working. Badgering, begging, shaming or guilting your partner to stay only demonstrates the intractable nature of your self-serving, controlling behavior, the very behavior from which your partner seeks relief.

Any semblance of a relationship you might hope for will be determined by the challenge of letting go of your desire for unification, weighed against the risk of never realizing your goal. This might be your first magnanimous act as a reformed abuser and, while perhaps too late for the present relationship, might give you a chance at a satisfying subsequent relationship. Remember, you cannot chase your partner all the while saying you now respect his or her right to make his or her own decisions. If there is any hope to rekindle a mutually satisfying relationship, you will have to let go of your demands.

Even if your partner does not want an intimate relationship with you, if you make the necessary changes, you still might enjoy a better co-parent relationship and your children will be better served. Your children can be spared becoming jerks or wimps as portrayed by their parents. Your behavior will continue to factor into their futures. Your successful treatment will create better conditions for them. The degree to which you, as a violent partner, can take responsibility for your attitude and behavior gives you the opportunity for a more mutually satisfying and successful relationship, but there is much to learn.

Assuming you do take this on, you can distinguish yourself from those who don't. You can present yourself as a caring but misguided partner versus a partner who is only evil. If you are caring but misguided, then in doing the work and making substantive changes you have a chance at a better life and relationship. It must be noted, though, that just doing the work is meaningless in the absence of change. Your basic makeup as a person and your quality of relationships will continue to be determined by behavior, not intention.

Perhaps you are beginning to see the harm your behavior has imposed. Take that feeling, take that glimmer of insight and get help. If you don't know where to begin, ask your physician, contact your local YMCA about community resources, inquire at your local family counseling agency or, if you have been in trouble with the law, discuss it with your probation officer or contact your nearest John Howard Society, a social service agency assisting those who have had conflicts with the law.

The coercive, violent behavior noted is only one type of violence It tends to garner the major share of attention because of the abject harm it imposes on victims. It is the kind of violence that most leads the victims, often women, to seek the safety of a shelter. From a physical perspective it tends to be the most dangerous kind of violence. It can create mental health issues in the form of anxiety and depression, can lead to hospitalization for injuries and can cause death.

But there are other contexts in which violence in a relationship can occur where the intent is not domination and control but where violent behavior can still lead to risk of harm.

Stuart and Elaine's Story

Stuart and Elaine were tight as a couple. Neither ever strayed; they had each other's back. They enjoyed a joint income, had a nice home and loved their two children.

Their elder son, Jason, age eight, often had stomachaches. Elaine took Jason to see the doctor on several occasions but no physical basis for the stomachaches was detected. The physician suggested counseling. Elaine called a local counselor who asked to meet with both parents ahead of meeting their son, explaining that there was developmental and family information to obtain to prepare for meeting with Jason. Elaine spoke with Stu who, although he did not understand the necessity of both parents attending, agreed to go with his wife.

As well as obtaining a developmental and family history, the counselor sought to understand how Stu and Elaine resolved conflict. At first they were defensive, telling the counselor they had a good relationship. The counselor pressed on: "Do you always agree on everything? What happens when you disagree?"

Stu and Elaine were prone to yelling at each other when in conflict. There were also the occasional incidents when Elaine threw a dish or Stu slammed a door. They were adamant that neither child ever heard their disputes, that the kids were asleep whenever their parents were "resolving conflict." There was nothing otherwise inappropriate in Jason's developmental background or the family history. The counselor agreed to meet with Jason at the next appointment, along with both parents.

After introductions and a chance for the counselor to develop some rapport with Jason and still in the company of his parents, the counselor started to ask him more probing questions. "Do you ever worry about your parents? Do you ever hear them argue? Are you ever worried someone could get hurt?"

It turned out that when Jason's parents thought he was asleep, he really crept to the top of the stairs and listened to their conversations. He was monitoring for raised voices. Jason recounted the night when he was awakened by the sound of a crash. The next morning he saw the bloodied towel in the kitchen trash and he noticed the bandage on his father's forehead. He had thought it weird at the time how his parents acted differently that morning, all nice.

That was the beginning of his concern for his parents. From then on, each night Jason spent the first half hour of his bedtime at the top of the stairs monitoring his parents. When asked what he did when he heard them arguing, Jason answered, "I go downstairs and say I have a stomachache. That way they concentrate on me and stop fighting."

The counselor advised Jason that she would take on the task of worrying about his parents so he could concentrate on getting a good night's sleep. Jason was satisfied and his parents promised to continue to meet with the counselor to address their issues. Stu and Elaine had several more sessions with the counselor learning how to manage their conflicts and eventually Jason's stomachaches disappeared.

It wasn't that their marriage was in tatters, but the manner in which Stu and Elaine resolved conflict created anxiety for Jason, causing him to feel responsible for their safety and well-being. Even though many parents are of the opinion that their children are not exposed to hurtful, harmful, violent behavior, the truth is that most children are exposed, if not by seeing the behavior, then by hearing it or witnessing the aftermath, such as observing injuries, altered or distraught moods, broken or destroyed objects, holes in walls and doors off hinges.

Exposure to these domestic events creates distress in children that can result in worry and anxiety. Some children have trouble concentrating at school, feel responsible and try to intervene on behalf of their parents' well-being. Even Derek from the earlier example sought to intervene on behalf of his mother's safety when he assaulted his father.

PARENT PATTERNS

Children are affected by the manner in which parents resolve their issues. Parents are children's training ground by way of observational learning. Through their parents children learn either how to get along well with others or not; they develop a sense of trust and calm in the world or view the world as a dangerous place. Depending on what they learn growing up in the context of the family, children enter the greater world with that as their frame of reference and their behavior reflects those lessons. If the world is not to be trusted, then children learn to hold back. If they learn the world is a good and giving place, then children become giving and generous.

As they exemplify what they have learned from their parents, they will typically be treated in kind. Enter the world with suspicion and worry, either holding back or seeking to get yours before another does, then you bring to a relationship any number of issues that can sabotage the integrity of that relationship. Bring a sense of trust and compassion built on the experiences of parents resolving conflict peacefully to everyone's satisfaction and you can develop adult relationships of similar quality.

Now is the time to reflect more fully on your upbringing. How did your parents resolve conflict? Was there yelling and screaming, pushing and shoving, hitting and punching, throwing and breaking, silence and withholding, running and hiding, lying and cheating? Now look at your current relationship. Are there similarities?

What if Stu and Elaine were stuck in a pattern where both felt they had to outdo the other; where when one won the conflict, the other felt he or she had to win the next battle; where one eventually got ticked off with the other? What if, during a pushing and shoving match in the heat of an argument, one lost his or her footing? What if it occasioned an unintentional fall down the stairs? What if one broke his or her neck?

Many people will see themselves in these descriptors and how their escalations of conflict can reach dangerous proportions. Some might be reflecting on holes in walls, broken doors, damaged heirlooms, smashed cell phones. Others might be thinking about partners who give the "silent treatment," don't seem to fight back, withdraw or walk away.

Think about a relationship in which you feel an intensity of anger and in which you harbor resentment. The thing about resentment is that it always seeks resolution. No one likes to hold on to the feeling of resentment. The trouble is that some people discharge resentment through retribution—getting someone back. A vicious cycle develops and continues: resentment, retribution, revenge. This is a two-sided street that both partners walk and is different from the coercive, one-sided type of violence where one partner seeks to dominate and control the other solely for his or her gratification. In this situation, both are involved and both have difficulty marshaling the type of maturity that can create the kind of win/win scenario that would prove mutually acceptable or the sort of maturity that conveys that partners can take turns.

As human beings, we can be greedy, needy, stingy, selfish and self-righteous. We might see the world as having limited resources, believe our needs should come ahead of others and incorrectly perceive others to have these traits, which in truth may originate in us. These issues can interfere with the integrity of our intimate relationships to differing extents. We lose perspective and may not possess the maturity or skills to resolve differences before they lead to conflict or may not have the ability to avoid conflict before someone gets hurt. Assuming you do not mean to hurt your partner yet have, look at your behavior and ask yourself: *Why wasn't I able to resist fighting? Why wasn't I able to discuss matters more reasonably? Why do I think I must win? What bad thing would happen if I was to give in? Why can't I generate alternative solutions where we both can feel satisfied? Why do I resist taking turns? Why am I apt to seek revenge over understanding? Why do I resort to violence?*

If you are prone to conflict or are in a relationship marked by conflict or violence and cannot answer these questions or discuss them with your partner, then seek help. If you find yourself fighting the same fight over and over or seeking to resolve matters the same way repeatedly with no resolution, then seek help.

Remember the definition of *crazy* from the first sin: Crazy is doing the same thing over and over again and expecting a different result. Hurting another repeatedly with or without apology will never produce a satisfying relationship. Trying the same old thing repeatedly with poor results will never foster a good relationship.

DOING THINGS DIFFERENTLY

To cease hurting your significant other and, by extension, yourself with a fractured and unsatisfying relationship, you need to learn more about yourself and your upbringing. You need to develop reasonable conflict resolution strategies and a more long-term perspective when you think you must win on every matter. Realize that there is more than one way to arrive at a destination. As you problem solve effectively and come to acknowledge each other's needs, you will learn there are enough resources for both of you. As you learn these things, you can stop applying the same ineffective strategies that you were using repeatedly which only caused you to feel crazy. If you want a different outcome, you must do something different to achieve it. Here are some ways to make things different:

- Cease sarcasm
- Attend a group for anger management
- Stop violence in any form for any reason
- Learn to express yourself to your partner non-accusatorily, non-defensively and informatively
- Learn to meta-communicate
- Apologize
- Take responsibility
- Make amends

- Take assertiveness training
- Attend individual or couples counseling
- Put your partner first
- Take a time-out if necessary
- Learn to manage stress
- Address other areas of concern, be they financial, extended kin or work

If you are being hurt or are doing the hurting, seek to do something different, non-injurious in any form, and see what happens. This is how to cease feeling and acting crazy.

ANALYSIS OF CASE STUDIES

Nadia's behavior hurt her husband and their children. Whether or not Nadia realized it, her husband did. It was incumbent on him to do something about it, to take some form of action, but he felt no match for Nadia. Phillip should ask Nadia to join him in couples therapy where he would have the support of a counselor to address his upset with Nadia and Nadia would also have support to process her husband's concerns. If Nadia declined to attend counseling with him, then he could go alone to learn how to assert himself and raise issues and start discussions with her. Running, hiding or avoiding rarely change anything. They help perpetuate the problem and many of these kinds of problems only worsen with time. Resentment and distance build, leaving only a sham of a relationship.

Even though many might blame Nadia for her obvious verbal/emotional abuse disguised as humor, some responsibility falls on her husband, whose inaction doesn't help the situation. Remember the sinner's motto *It's not me; it's you*? Nadia's husband has a role to play and he needs to take responsibility for the problem as does Nadia. Waiting for her to do something different won't work. Phillip can take action to bring about a different result. He can stop running and hiding, doing the same old thing. He can work to rescue his marriage and, in this case, his daughter too. If you are like Nadia's husband, look for help either as a couple or on an individual basis. Do not start with the premise, "My partner has a problem," but rather with the premise, "I don't know how to express myself under duress. I don't know how to assert myself."

If you, like Derek, are a violent, self-centered partner, you need to mend your ways. Behaving like Derek can lead to criminal offenses, incarceration, job loss and the end of one's marriage as well as impact heavily on one's relationship with one's children. Partners with a propensity to violence on average have more limited or even no access to their children. If violent means are the only strategies you have to achieve your goals and you want to avoid the consequences of your behavior, then learn to manage yourself differently.

As you act more reasonably, even if in your own self-interest, you can be perceived as a better partner for your significant other and a better parent to your children. This can lead to a more peaceful existence where your needs are more appropriately met even if your underlying attitudes remain. While not making for the best of outcomes, it may make your relationship salvageable. Despite the fact that many people might find this repulsive, improving yourself solely for your own sake and somewhat manipulatively to maintain your relationship, this may be good enough for your partner. To stay or go remains your partner's decision even if others may find staying unattractive.

If you, like Joanne, are a meek partner, get counseling from someone with knowledge, training and experience in the area of domestic violence or intimate partner violence. This may be through a local counseling agency, your employee benefit plan, a counselor in private practice or a local women's shelter. It is vital that the counselor you see is a qualified individual who has the required knowledge and experience; otherwise, you could be at risk of greater harm. Without knowledge and experience, your counselor may not understand or appreciate the danger of your situation and, as a result, may offer solutions that could create greater risk of harm. While a free service may sound attractive, a less-than-adequate or inappropriate service (at any price) is not worth the consequences. Be prepared to ask any service provider about his or her qualifications, training and experience in the area of domestic violence. If this person does not provide sufficient evidence of the necessary skills, move on. Not all counselors possess this knowledge and training, because this is a specialized area.

Stu and Elaine are squabblers, people who bicker about anything. Conflict is a way of life for them. Eventually people get tired of the constant wrangling and seek to change it. It more often starts with one spouse, the one who feels life is too short for this kind of thing. This person raises his or her head from the fray and tries to bring the issue to a head by saying, "Enough. We/I can't go on this way."

BREAKING THE CONFLICT CYCLE

If conflict has been a way of life for the couple, it is unlikely the partners will oblige easily; instead, this serves as the new object of dispute. Whether spouses fight too much becomes a fight itself. Even though you have tired of it and want it to end, your partner isn't to that point yet. Your partner may be oblivious to the extent of your discontent, given your history together as squabblers. To your partner, voicing your discontent might make you look crazy, both for doing the same old thing and for behaving in a manner of which you are critical. You look hypocritical and the battle intensifies.

The only way to resolve this differently is to disengage, stop the fighting, even if only on a one-sided basis. This is a tug of war, with both sides pulling on a rope between them. As each tries to win, both tighten their grips. You are locked in a battle with no resolution. If you lose the current battle, you take up the rope on the next issue so as to even the score and not lose the war. There are only two ways to end a tug of war: you both lay down the rope together or one side lets go unilaterally. If you cannot get your partner to lay down the rope together, you will have to let go by yourself. Don't fight back.

Disengage. You can let your partner know that you are not prepared to fight any longer and that for those things you cannot resolve together, you will make a unilateral decision where possible. Your partner might complain that you have gone your own way, which is correct. But if your partner isn't pleased with that outcome, you could ask your partner if a more mutually acceptable solution could be achieved, such as attending counseling with the view to learning how to make joint decisions that both partners could support. With your partner destabilized by your letting go of the rope, it is hoped your partner will be amenable to changing the usual routine.

Remember our discussion about the developmental psychologist Erik Erikson? We took a look at the whole of the human lifespan. He spoke of integrity versus despair at the final stage of life and helped us to understand that, at some point, we will be taking stock of our lives, assessing from our ledger and hoping the good outweighs the bad. Squabblers should remember this, because so much of what squabblers argue about is inconsequential. They must learn to take a long-term view of their disputes in terms of impact upon the relationship and how to assess the issues of their disagreement to determine if the dispute is really consequential. As squabblers learn to cease this behavior, they also learn to put things in appropriate perspective and to prioritize their relationships ahead of winning a trite dispute.

Many social workers, psychologists, psychiatrists and other mental health professionals discuss compromise as a means to resolve conflict and maintain the integrity and satisfaction of an intimate relationship. But compromise isn't always the best method. As I said earlier, compromise often entails giving something up in order to achieve something else. Compromise implies a cost/benefit analysis where the partners subject to the compromise must consider what is lost against what is gained. Even if it is a rational decision, compromise always entails some degree of dissatisfaction or loss. For that reason, as previously indicated, I prefer priorities. If your relationship is your priority and your decisions play to that priority, then you never lose. You are always winning in terms of your priority, the relationship.

If you don't mean to hurt someone, then don't. Rather than hurting, elevate your partner's needs and wants above your own. This should be the reciprocal nature of your relationship where you both act and feel like each other's priority. Prepare now so that when you die, you do so with integrity—an intact, mutually satisfying relationship, true to the end.

The Winner's Motto:
We respect each other as our mutual priority.

Making Your Children the Problem

The Sinner's Motto:
Children are a pain.

O ur formative experiences as children growing up within our families shape our adult lives. The Lebanese-American poet Kahlil Gibran wrote in his book *The Prophet*, "You are the bows from which your children as living arrows are sent forth."

As we did with our parents, our children learn to cope, relate and problem solve based on what they observe in us. This is internalized and follows them through childhood and adolescence and into adulthood where they put their experiences and observational knowledge into practice within their intimate relationships. Parental behavior is more than influential; it is predictive. Even if children try to do the opposite of what they learned by observing their parents, they are still choosing behavior in relation to what they learned and thus are still influenced by it. Be aware that you, as a parent, set the trajectory for your children's lives. The challenge is to provide the best for your children while not exposing them to the untoward behavior to which you may have been exposed as a child.

In some cases we want to change the trajectory of our children's path from one generation to the next. While we are the bow, developed from the arrow of our past, we as adults can make decisions, choices. We can learn to behave differently. We can give our children a future different from our past. This is the story of immigrants who come to a new country for better opportunities. They want to change their children's trajectory by offering something that they didn't have when they were growing up. This is also the story of the impoverished who become educated to achieve better-paying jobs and escape the cycle of poverty. While our past may not be undone, we can choose to view it anew, more maturely and with deeper and greater perspective through which we make different decisions for the care of our young, all so that their trajectory can be better or easier than our own.

How spouses parent and provide for the care of their youngsters can cause dissension in relationships. So too can the decision or lack of decision by which they enter into having children. Apart from raising children is also the issue of parenting another person's children—stepchildren. Children, whether or not to have them, how we decide, whose they are and how we care for them, can be a serious cause for distress in marriages and relationships.

Carey and Dan's Story

Carey and Dan met one night at a bar. Both were drinking and both had recently-exited relationships. They noticed each other when chatting with friends nearby. There was a spark, some chemistry, something in the air that night that created a tension, an obvious attraction. They spoke, giggled and laughed. She flipped her hair and he touched her arm.

They spent that night together at his apartment and they had sex. In the morning she left, unsure of herself. She had never done that before; it was a first.

Over the next few days Carey and Dan talked, texted and chatted, but somehow the spark wasn't there anymore. It had felt great in the moment and helped squelch the pain of relationships recently lost but it wasn't the start of anything new, just a fun diversion, a fling.

A few weeks went by and Carey realized something was missing. At first she tried to pretend she forgot her dates, but with the passing of another few weeks, she could no longer deny she had missed her period.

When the pregnancy was confirmed, she was in a quandary. Terrified by the pregnancy, she secretly contemplated its termination; then she came to believe the pregnancy was a good thing. She decided she would not have an abortion and would keep the baby.

Feeling a sense of responsibility, she spoke with Dan and broke the news. Dan was adamant that she get an abortion. The pregnancy was unplanned, they barely knew each other and neither was prepared to become a parent. What Dan didn't realize was that Carey's decision to keep the child was an investment in her own fantasy of what was to come. She envisioned a life with this baby, a life that would complete her own, a life that would be fulfilling. She was prepared to go it alone. Telling Dan was a courtesy. She wasn't looking for anything in return.

Once Dan accepted Carey's decision, he told his parents, who were deeply antagonistic and angry. He could feel his parents watching him, judging him. Even though he had entered into a drunken sexual encounter, he had been raised in a wholesome home. His guilt overtook him and he felt compelled to do the right thing by Carey and raise the child with her.

Carey was uncertain at first. Dan had originally pressed for an abortion. What kind of father could he, who at first thought of killing his unborn child, be? She dismissed her own similar thoughts when she was first confronted with the pregnancy. Her uncertainty gave way to her fantasy of an intact, two-parent family. They didn't marry but agreed to date and eventually began living together just before the child was due to be born.

CHOICE AND CHANCE

What happens when we take the element of choice from our lives, when we cannot choose our own destinies, when we cannot determine our fates? Can we go passively into the future? Do we remain flexible and adaptive or do we become bitter and resentful? And when we were participants in causing that fate, a fate unanticipated or unwanted, then what? What if our fate is intertwined with someone else whose behavior and choices comingle with our own to produce an unplanned event? Do we settle? Do we blame and project responsibility for the outcome onto the other? Do we embrace our fate and meet that which was created, without intent, with purpose and determination? Can we learn to love another in a partnership of circumstance?

Predictably, Carey and Dan have much to get used to: An unplanned pregnancy, an originally unwanted child, a decision to maintain the pregnancy and a decision to make a relationship between two people whose life together began with no meaningful knowledge of each other. This could be a relationship fraught with all sorts of conflict seated in resentment from lack of choice, the kind of conflict that comes from mashing two incompatible initial desires together to work as one.

Making a decision to keep and raise the child together doesn't mean Dan and Carey will like it. When the going gets tough, how will those initial feelings be revisited and thrust upon each other and even upon the child? Will the child grow to be the brunt of unresolved resentment? If so, how will that reflect in parenting decisions and the care of the child? Can one love a child whose emergence connects one to a partner not of one's choosing?

How do Carey and Dan prepare for the birth? Do they attend prenatal classes together? Is Dan present for the delivery? Do they make choices together with respect to breastfeeding, diaper changes, nighttime feedings, sleep, crib, infant carriers, bathing?

Do Carey and Dan have sex? Have they had sex beyond that one fateful evening? With the birth of the child and care of the child, is sex a possibility? Are they comfortable with the thought of sex, given what it led to before? Are they practicing birth control? Is Carey fatigued from the birth and care of the baby? Is Dan stressed about work and making ends meet? How are Dan and Carey managing their financial obligations and how have they divvied up the cost of living with each other and caring for the baby? Have they discussed any of this? Do they know each other's preferences or expectations?

Are any of Dan's or Carey's parents involved? Will their parents accept their son's and daughter's decisions given the behavior that initiated their situation? Will their respective parents get along with their child's new partner? Can Dan's and Carey's parents overlook how their relationship came to be and develop good rapport in a respectful environment? How do Dan and Carey feel about each other's parents? Are they welcome in the home? Do they have good boundaries or do any of them seem intrusive?

Given all the issues Carey and Dan are facing, do you think they will make it as a couple? Do you see yourself in their story? Have you even begun to contemplate the myriad issues befalling them? Does reading about the issues faced by Dan and Carey give you some insight as to what may be contributing to a problem in your own relationship? If your relationship is long term, can you honestly say that these early relationship and parenting issues have been resolved or are they creating obstacles to the resolution of newer problems imposed by a different stage of child and family development?

Has an unplanned pregnancy been the first in a series of issues, cascading to create one bad outcome after another, or have you been able to sit down and put all these issues on the table for a discussion leading to some degree of resolution? Is it time to reflect with your partner about the circumstances of your getting together and address unresolved resentment? Is it time to start leading your life by intent versus accident? Is it time to plan, using now as a starting point to chart a path for a more reasonable direction?

Love can grow from a place where love wasn't found before. Parents can and do learn to separate the circumstances of their child's emergence from their love for that child and advance the needs of the child over their own wants or desires. Even though a pregnancy is unplanned, you can have the relationship and the family you dreamed of, but it will take considerably more work and patience than if you entered into this life by design. It will take considerable maturity and patience.

FACING FEARS

You and your partner have a child and the process of conception in common. You already have a great deal to talk about, particularly if you give yourselves the freedom, the permission, to speak candidly about your fears, initial impressions and thoughts. This will require the kind of permission where what is revealed out of fear is not held against either person. Do not judge based on what a person feels as the result of fear. Thoughts are a psychological coping mechanism to relieve the distress of fear. Even if your partner's initial reaction was to want an abortion, he or she was scared and worried about a life not chosen, the attitudes of loved ones, one's own behavior and responsibility, personal shame and embarrassment. Abortion is not an unnatural thought or discussion point; it is within the range of outcomes to the situation of an unplanned, unwanted pregnancy. Even if contradictory to one's faith, one might still contemplate solutions that once would never have been entertained.

With fear, our thoughts may turn to dark places and we may be overwhelmed. Thoughts bring some sense of psychological reprieve to fear. We talk about fear to release it and allow for more effective problem solving. Through discussion, it is hoped we come to a solution we can accept, though not necessarily like.

You and your partner have much in common: your initial behavior, your thoughts, your discussions, your decisions, your actions. And you have still more to talk about. As you continue to talk you develop your shared history and it is that which you have in common at the start of your journey.

SHARED HISTORY

Your limited shared history may be marred by upset, by the situation, by one's reaction, by one's extended family and other factors. If you learn to talk about the upset without the blame and just bear witness to the concerns of the other person, non-judgmentally and without seeking immediate resolution, you will become supportive of each other.

Even though Dan and Carey entered into therapy regarding their different approaches to getting their now two-year-old daughter to sleep in her own bed and to toilet train, it was clear to the therapist that they were stuck as a couple on issues from when they first got together. The therapist they consulted about their child understood that the unresolved issues of both parents were mixed in with their parenting decisions and although they didn't enter therapy to address their relationship, the relationship was at the root of their parenting problems.

Carey and Dan hadn't had discussions that led to resolution. They never admitted their fears. They hadn't learned to speak freely, without judgment, to feel mutually heard and supported. They did not know each other's views and fears, preferences and expectations, competencies and capacities. They only knew the behavior of unresolved fear and perhaps resentment given the fear. They were apt to rush to solutions that only gave rise to new fears.

Carey and Dan's therapist had them start by saying to each other, "I don't really know you and I am locked in a lifelong relationship with you, if only as co-parent. I am scared by this: not knowing who you are; not knowing if we are compatible; not knowing if we share similar values; not knowing if we would raise a child the same; not knowing how we will sort out our differences."

This ignorance of each other was Carey and Dan's ongoing problem. With their daughter in the bed, Carey was spared the thought of sex. Carey coddled her daughter and projected that Dan was bad, because he wanted to push their daughter out of their bed to an empty room of her own. Carey thought him heartless.

Dan sought to prove his parenting prowess by showing Carey that he could toilet train their daughter. Carey objected. He couldn't fathom why Carey would want her daughter to remain a baby in diapers.

In the scheme of things, having a child sleep in her own room is not much of a challenge when both parents are resolved to see that happen. A child who exhibits the signs of readiness for toileting typically learns with little fuss, particularly when the parents share a similar approach and are patient with their little one.

The therapist probed the context of Dan and Carey's relationship as well as their thoughts and feelings regarding the course of their time together and the responses and reactions of friends and family. Fortunately, neither Carey nor Dan objected and in the process they learned things about each other they never knew. They learned of each other's initial fears, dreams and aspirations. They realized that both were good listeners and this brought them closer together.

After learning about each other, they then discussed how to set mutual goals and how to plan to achieve those goals. They began to accommodate each other. The initial issues with their daughter sleeping in their bed and toilet training seemed to dissipate on their own.

Dan and Carey were not inherently bad people, just frightened and anxious. Time in the therapist's office allowed them

to come together. They learned to manage adversity and make
something positive of it. This proved satisfying and it was what
they had in common. With that they were able to adjust and ap-
preciate each other and they came to love each other.

CONFLICTED PARENTING

Some couples are in conflict over their respective parenting styles. One parent seeks to be understanding while the other seeks to be punitive. The parent who is understanding is seen as a pushover by the parent who is punitive and the parent who is punitive is seen as abusive by the parent who is understanding. Children learn to ride the wedge of parental differences to get what they want. The children win but at the expense of the parents' relationship and with an escalation of conflict over parenting styles.

Larry and Leticia's Story

Larry and Leticia, both in their early forties, had two sons, Samuel, ten, and Scott, eight. Scott was well liked by everyone. He was a good-natured boy who did what he was told, who didn't get into trouble and earned good grades.

His older brother Samuel was the opposite. Samuel goofed off, didn't apply himself at school and liked to push the limits. He loved to get his own way and he whined, begged, demanded, talked back and became obstinate until he did. Bedtime was never bedtime. Meals were catered to his wants. The TV reflected his choice of channel. Samuel was a stubborn child. He frustrated his father. His mother did his bidding and kept his father at a distance, making excuses for Samuel that only helped fuel the boy's self-serving disposition and demanding behavior.

Leticia sought to shelter Samuel from his father's temper, never realizing Larry's temper was fueled further by her constant giving in to Samuel.

Larry believed Leticia was creating the problems to which he objected. He thought Leticia spoiled their son and was turning him into a brat.

Leticia's understanding of the situation was different from Larry's. She believed she was only protecting Samuel and compensating for Larry's harsh discipline. At times she thought Larry was abusive and so Samuel deserved special attention.

When they tried to discuss their respective positions, Leticia twisted everything around, saying Larry's harsh approach created Samuel's rebellious nature. Larry didn't want to be perceived as a bad guy, so he begrudgingly acquiesced to Leticia's point of view. Neither parenting style was especially bad on its own, but in combination they co-created an awful dynamic.

When Samuel was carrying on to get his way and running roughshod over his mother, Larry verbally rebuked Samuel, threatening to either spank him or send him to his room. In Larry's mind, there was no way Samuel was going to get away with that bad behavior. Larry was going to teach Samuel a lesson and compensate for Leticia's always giving in.

That was when Leticia ran to Samuel's defense, forgetting Samuel's behavior to concentrate on Larry's reaction. She negotiated his intended punishment to the point where his father apologized to Samuel for his harsh behavior. Samuel wound up getting his way in the end, kind of like a reward for having been subject to his father's severe ways. Superficially, Samuel looked contrite as Larry blamed Samuel for bringing on his threatening behavior.

Samuel knew he would get what he wanted and escape punishment. Samuel was so good at it that he could look contrite while gazing at his parents and then have a devilish smirk when looking over at someone else, signaling that he was the master manipulator.

Larry and Leticia see-sawed back and forth between being overly punitive and being overly understanding. Larry, though, was acting more like an abusive father. One day Samuel cursed at his father. Larry struck Samuel and gave him a black eye.

The next day Samuel's teacher, seeing his black eye and hearing his version of the story, called child protective services. The worker from child protective services heard the story from the teacher, with the message: mother good, father bad. With Larry's place in the home threatened and their marriage finally disintegrating, Larry and Leticia were compelled to attend couples therapy.

DIVERSE PARENTING STYLES

Parenting styles exist on a continuum. Many parents juggle understanding versus punishment as means to address troublesome child behavior. As they pull in opposite directions, each believes he or she must try harder to undo the impact of the other. As their parenting becomes the battleground, the child's behavior is not addressed and the child instinctively learns how to manipulate the parental differences to get what he or she wants. This situation is poisonous for a marriage and for the child's socialization.

AUTHORITARIAN PARENTING

On one end of the continuum is authoritarian parenting. Authoritarian parenting is marked by an approach that is demanding, with little room for discussion or negotiation: "You will do what you are told…or else." The authoritarian parent is the boss and the child must do as expected or face consequences. Step out of line and the child's behavior is met with punishment. The child learns that to avoid bad consequences, he or she must do as told. The child internalizes, *Follow the rules or else.* This child grows up to be rule bound. Since the child's thinking is organized hierarchically, whoever is on top is the boss. Whoever is on top makes the rules and determines who gets what and when.

Whenever possible, as a child and as an adult, the person decides he or she must rule. If the child was exposed to parental abuse or harsh discipline as a means to gain or restore order and compliance, then he or she may adopt similar strategies to have his or her way in the playground, schoolyard, classroom and even in the family among siblings.

In some cases, other children, in order to get their way against the expectations of the authoritarian parent, may learn that being sneaky and hiding allows them to subvert parental authority. Among the families we discussed earlier, the sons and daughters often exhibited these behavioral styles. Samuel was overtly oppositional to his father's authority and chose to stay close to his mother to override his father. In contrast, Scott's overt good behavior may have been the shroud he cloaked himself in to get away with things beyond detection. Children of authoritarian parents learn to internalize structure and self-discipline, but it is the kind that is designed to avoid consequences. Their behavior is less about doing good to others and more about avoidance of personal trouble. Compliance is based on a self-serving cost/benefit analysis. To survive a demanding, authoritarian parent, these children learn to submit, choose oppositional strategies or be sneaky.

PERMISSIVE PARENTING

On the other end of the parenting continuum is permissive parenting. Permissive parents usually do not view themselves as permissive, because they actually view themselves as having expectations. The issue, though, isn't whether a parent has expectations but hinges upon the parent holding the child accountable to those expectations. The parent who tells his or her child to behave, to go to bed on time, to clean up after him or herself yet doesn't follow through to see that the child meets the expectation, or caves against the objection, manipulation or contrary behavior of the child is practicing permissive parenting. Permissive parenting also includes parents who do not have expectations, handle their children's needs, engage appropriately in the care of the children or hold children accountable to reasonable expectations. These parents are permissive by omission and neglect-ful by extension. Their children do not finish their schoolwork, do not have set bedtimes, come home late and have no chores or need for part-time jobs and the parents don't seem to care.

Children who learn to undermine a parent's expectations come to believe they can always have their own way. When they don't get what they want, they protest by ramping up the strategies that have worked in the past. If whining worked in a previous situation, the child whines louder. If crying and temper tantrums once got results, the child cries harder. If hitting worked in the past, the child hits harder. Children of permissive parents appear self-centered, because they frequently get their way even if their demands are not good for them. These children grow up to believe they can do what they want, when they want, and they do not feel bound by any particular set of rules or even laws. These children believe that they can talk their way out of anything. They are manipulative brats, at least to others except the permissive parent.

Samuel was a master at getting his own way with his permissive mother in defiance of the demands of his authoritarian father. Samuel and Scott's mother, Leticia, had minimal expectations. Scott's strategy of staying close to her, not overtly working against either parent, spared him detection from his father and allowed him to get away with things in a somewhat more sophisticated manner than his older brother, Samuel.

PARENTING CONFLICT

If parents have the same parenting styles, either authoritarian or permissive, they usually concur and handle their children's discipline. Assuming the parents are not so far at either end of the continuum to create a disturbance, there would be no issue about discipline between them and no parental/marital conflict. If, however, they are so authoritarian so as to be abusive or so permissive as to be neglectful, then trouble could surface and would be reflected in their children's behavior and safety, but they would still be fine as a couple, because they would be supportive of each other, parenting from the same viewpoint. These parents see no wrong in themselves for their parenting, the result of being united in style. They will agree that their child deserved a wallop or that their child deserved his or her freedom, resulting in truancy or some similar problem, depending on which end of the continuum from which they parent.

If two parents come from opposite ends of the parenting continuum, they are ripe for conflict. They will have opposing opinions when addressing most childhood issues and the child, exposed to these parental differences, can learn to exploit the parents. These children grow up to subvert authority and their strategies range the gamut from aggression to obeying only the necessary rules to utilizing virtually any means to undo expectations. These children appear pseudo-caring and concerned. They use their skills to pull at the heartstrings of one parent to advocate against the other. They pit people against each other, exploiting individual differences to meet their own desires. Their hapless victims are left arguing with each other, rather than addressing the behavior of the initiator of their conflict. Parental conflict serves this child: he or she hides behind the conflict, doing what he or she wants, contrary to the parents' wishes, expectations or awareness.

Larry and Leticia did not see Samuel's problem coming. They had no idea that what started as minor differences would intensify over time, leading one parent to be abusive and the other parent to be permissive. Both denied their parenting styles and contribution to distress. Both believed their parenting and marital problems originated solely with the other partner. When abuse becomes a factor, though, it is difficult to step back and look at the broader dynamics and contribution of both parents. Unless Larry's behavior is addressed in the context of a clash of opposing parenting styles, the likelihood of repairing Larry and Leticia's relationship is minimal. Unless Larry's behavior is analyzed in a way that includes Leticia's parenting style, the odds of reining in Samuel's bad behavior is poor.

AUTHORITATIVE PARENTING

To resolve this kind of relationship problem, both parents will have to come to terms with their respective parenting styles and learn a cooperative form of parenting called authoritative parenting. Although similar sounding to authoritarian parenting, authoritative parenting is different.

Flexible and nurturing, an authoritative parent also has expectations and holds a child accountable to those expectations. This parent engages the child in the setting of expectations, the means of accountability and the strategy for effecting the desired objective. For instance, while the child has to go to bed at a certain time, it can remain negotiable whether one parent reads a story, when the child's teeth are brushed and whether the child eats a snack. The parents can discuss exactly what time the child's bedroom lights go out versus what time the child goes to bed. Parents do not have to dictate all the terms or set out all the requirements to accomplish a task or expectation. Parents adopting this middle, authoritative style know that their child can participate in the process and that, along the way, the parents will demonstrate kind, loving and supportive behaviors. No abuse, no caving in.

Children of parents who are fair can grow up to be reasonable people. They will know they cannot always get their own ways and will be prepared to discuss issues to bring about resolutions acceptable to all involved. These children learn that there are limits in life. Because their parents are reasonable, they won't worry about getting their own way every time. They have at times experienced negotiating and find their parents to be fair and balanced. These children make good friends and intimate partners. They have good senses of justice, fairness and group interest over self-interest.

COOPERATIVE PARENTING

If you are in conflict with your partner over parenting styles, as difficult as it may be to resist admonishing your partner for his or her style, you must do so in favor of reviewing your own. It is very often the case that when one seems abusive or harsh, the other is extremely permissive. You will both need to moderate your parenting approaches to come toward the middle of the parenting continuum. This is of vital importance when your relationship is conflicted because of differing parenting styles. You and your partner must be agreeable about a parenting method. This may involve taking parenting classes. Attending these classes can be very therapeutic for your relationship as well as good for the well-being of your children. Being "on the same page" will help you set standards and goals for your children and get along as a couple. You will no longer be subject to your child being pulled first one way and then another or pitting one parent against the other for the child's gain. You will learn to set and hold your child accountable to reasonable expectations. You can bring peace to your home and improve the social, academic, vocational and intimate outcome for your child.

Do not despair when you begin setting reasonable expectations and your child balks. You will have to anticipate your child's backlash; your child is used to using one parent against the other and coming up the winner. Your child won't want to lose this inappropriate position of power and so your child will utilize his or her full armature of resources. Whatever strategies your child has used in the past, expect him or her to employ them with greater intensity, frequency and duration. Your child may try harder, louder, more often and longer, all in an increased effort to undermine the new parental regime and restore the prior order. This escalation is not a signal that something is wrong, but that you and your partner are thwarting your child's efforts to get his or her way. Wear your child's protest as a badge of honor, all the while resisting your own escalation of prior harsh tactics or relinquishing control to appease the child. Remember to act in loving and caring ways while tolerating the child's protests. Show that these protests will not sway you from your expectations and that you can remain reasonable.

Leticia and Larry were challenged by learning a new parenting style. Larry readily accepted the realization that his behavior had been, at times, abusive, but he rejected the thought of being perceived as an abusive father. He sought a close relationship with his sons, Samuel and Scott.

Leticia was more defensive than Larry. Her challenge was the difficulty in accepting that she was permissive. She saw herself as caring and didn't like the thought of being complicit in a parenting dynamic contrary to her sons' well-being.

Leticia didn't realize her contribution to the marital distress, but because of Larry's behavioral changes, they moved forward. Because Leticia didn't take the work as meaningfully as Larry, the relationship didn't improve as much as it could have, but they were able to live together.

What if the children in question are not your own? What if they are the children of your partner and you are a stepparent? How does that figure into relationship difficulties?

Brian and Barbara's Story

Brian and Barbara both had children from their prior marriages. Barbara's children were eight and twelve, a girl and a boy, and Brian's children were nine and ten, both boys. Barbara's children lived with her and Brian; Brian's children visited every other weekend.

Barbara got along with her former husband and co-parented reasonably well with him. The way they handled the care of the children was pretty easy. They made arrangements between themselves and never through the children. The children had as much time with their father as either they or their father wanted.

Brian's marriage with his ex-wife was never good and since they didn't communicate, messages between them traveled through the children. Brian's former partner was concerned that Brian's new wife, Barbara, was getting into her business when it came to the children and often made demands, not considering Brian's or the children's desire to spend time together. Barbara felt that Brian was losing time with his children.

Brian was hands off when it came to Barbara's children. He wasn't one to jump in to help them out, play with them or check their homework. This irked Barbara, who wanted Brian to be more active as a stepparent. She also was frustrated with Brian's former partner, who acted angry every time Barbara did something nice for Brian's children.

Barbara pressed Brian to speak with his ex-wife about spending more time with his children. Brian felt he shouldn't upset his former partner. Additionally, when Brian's children did visit, they wreaked havoc in the house and upset Barbara's children.

Barbara phoned a therapist looking for help for Brian and his former partner so he could have more time with his children and his ex-wife wouldn't be so controlling. However, the therapist felt Barbara was the one in most distress and had much to sort out with her new partner, Brian. The therapist was prepared to work with Brian and Barbara if they were willing to undertake therapy.

Which part of Brian and Barbara's story seems like your own? Is your partner not engaging in the role of stepparent? Are you frustrated by your partner's ex-spouse? Is your current partner opinionated about your former relationship and ex-spouse's care of the children? Is the blending of two families not working? Is a former partner critical of you?

BLENDED FAMILIES

Step-families are like the Olympic rings: all intertwined. Each Olympic ring has a unique boundary and color, yet all are joined. Your newly blended family is the middle ring. Attached to either side are two more rings representing your children from a prior relationship and your partner's children from a former relationship. Joined to the rings representing your respective children are two more rings which represent the children's other parents and families. Note that the rings representing the children are connected to two families: your new one and the one of the other parent. Your children connect you to each other's former partner. This is the structural outcome of blended families.

The Olympic rings represent the five parts of the world coming together. Do all the parts of your world come together too? Getting involved with a partner who has children from a former relationship means you are connected to his or her former partner. Being an adult in the home where someone else's children are present means you have additional responsibilities. But what do those connections mean? How are they managed?

Partners in a blended family have a lot to talk about and much room for conflict. What are your responsibilities when it comes to the children of someone with whom you have a relationship? What are your expectations of each other in the context of a blended family and stepparenting? How do your expectations of each other mesh with the expectations or values of your former partner or your partner's former partner? If you have a problem, whose problem is it? Let's start by discussing that factor.

If you could pull on any of the Olympic rings, because they are connected, they all would move. Stepfamilies are the same, but perhaps a bit more elastic. A pull on any part of a stepfamily sends a wave of movement through the entire structure. Pull on any part too forcefully and the entire structure collapses. If one member of a stepfamily has a problem, it will likely be felt most forcefully within its immediate ring, but the reverberations will transfer along to the other rings. A problem in the middle ring might be felt equally in the outer rings and an issue originating in an outer ring may have only little impact by the time the reverberations transfer to the other side. Something that affects one member can transfer through the whole system.

A common issue in blended families is sorting out who spends what holidays and vacations with whom. How can your children and your partner's children be together for a certain holiday if your partner's former partner wants to see the children that same day too? Can you form a cohesive unit? Will all the children come together on the holiday? Will your investment in this outcome create distress that reverberates through the entire structure? Are you hammering your new partner to make this happen? Is your partner's former partner doing the hammering to meet this objective? Is this a tangled web of incompatible objectives? Are you out to win?

To sort things out, the perspective best taken is one that concerns the well-being of the children. Amid all the noise and confusion of blended family life, the single greatest determinant of the well-being of the children is freedom from parental or family conflict. The most important indicator of how well children will do as youngsters, adolescents and then adults is the degree of conflict to which they are exposed while growing up. The greater the conflict to which children are exposed, the more likely the children will have problems at school, with relationships, with behavior, with drugs and alcohol, in their jobs and in their intimate lives as adults.

Celebrating a holiday on a day other than the designated day will bring no harm as long as the decision is entered into with little to no conflict. Winning having the children celebrate a certain holiday at your house after a drawn-out, high-conflict court battle can seriously affect your children's future and your life-long relationship with them. Conflict matters to the long-term well-being of children; the day of celebrating a holiday doesn't. Many wise stepfamilies have opted to celebrate holidays when all can be together in the absence of conflict. Making a special day creates for these families and children their own traditions, which will carry them happily as a whole family into their future. Flexible thinking and planning help stepfamilies form that elusive cohesive unit.

FEELING VALUED

Remember the discussion on self-esteem and feeling valued? Apart from freedom from conflict, the next important thing, from a child's perspective, is feeling valued. We all want and need to be loved, cared for, adored, made to feel special and made to feel important. Meeting this inherent need to feel valued creates a sense of contentment in children with which they can go on to address other developmental tasks. Feeling content with oneself, one is ready to improve competencies academically, athletically, artistically and socially. Feeling good and secure with him or herself and without the distractions of conflict, the child has the wherewithal to concentrate on these other matters and develop.

The most important contributors to a child's well-being, freedom from conflict and feeling valued, come from those who are most important to the child, parents and stepparents. Because fathers generally have less time with their own children than they might with their stepchildren, men often worry that special occasions directed toward their stepchildren might be negatively interpreted by their natural children. The concern is that when a parent has and spends more time with and develops a caring relationship with stepchildren, the biological children might feel that parent doesn't care for them or cares less for them. So while Mom wants Stepfather to be more involved with her natural kids so they feel valued, Stepfather is worried that his involvement with his new wife's children will undermine his relationship to and the development of his own children. This creates a zero-sum situation where giving to one takes from the other.

The solution to the conundrum lies in communicating feelings and apprehensions through conversation.

CONVERSATION

Parents are best advised to discuss concerns with their children—step and natural—to make hidden feelings open and transparent. Parents must encourage their children's disclosure of perceptions and feelings. This can be facilitated by the parents expressing their concerns and asking their children questions to see if the concerns are shared.

This should not be done in such a way so as to lay blame on another or to make another feel responsible for improving the situation or another's feelings. It should be done to make covert feelings and concerns overt. The conversation should convey sentiments such as: "Let's communicate how each of us is feeling and why. Let's learn from each other how the situation and our decisions affect us without rushing to change things. Let's come to terms with our perceptions and feelings."

Only after you have fully explored and understand the range of your perceptions and feelings as well as your partner's can you begin to consider solutions, if any issues remain. At times, just surfacing perceptions and feelings leads to resolution. Other times the solution may be self-evident and it may be easily accomplished.

After such surfacing through conversation to generate solutions, any solution you come up with must be considered in the context of the five rings of your blended family and the reverberations from one ring to another. It may be that your power, authority, influence or ability to change anything is restricted to your own ring. If a better solution involves another ring, then you will have to invite the members of the other ring into the conversation in order to determine if you can gain support for your proposed solution.

As a result of inviting members from another ring into the conversation, you may find that your proposed solution creates negative reverberations elsewhere. It may be that your proposed solution either doesn't work or needs to be altered. Remember, flexible thinking and planning remain key. Through discussion, whereas you might have previously considered the members of another ring to be intransigent, you might now understand the forces at work that help you appreciate and come to terms with matters beyond your control and beyond the members of your own ring. Learning about each partner's challenges can create empathy, which in turn can reduce animosity and improve understanding and compassion. You might live more easily with a situation you had hoped would change once you understand what created it.

Taking on the process of conversation and problem solving by including both partners and children affected by the issue can lead to greater understanding and better commitment if a solution is accepted by all those who are subject to the solution. Using this format as opposed to fighting in court is more conciliatory, more reasonable, less combative. Recognizing that conflict is more destructive than most second-best solutions, you, your children and your stepchildren will know where everyone stands and why. The children will be spared the turmoil of being dragged into their parents' battle. No child wants either parent to be hurt physically, emotionally, psychologically, spiritually or financially. Children want the love and attention of their two intact parents.

If a better solution cannot be generated, then you need to learn to cope with matters beyond your control. By doing this you learn the world doesn't always provide for what you want. You learn to develop some degree of acceptance and tolerance. You learn to manage frustration. You find a way to make the best of a situation not of your choosing. Through it all, you let your children know you love them no matter what and that the time you do share together, you do so with a fully present mind not distracted by conflict.

Conflict for more time may win the quantum of time but at the expense of the relationship. If you do seek to dispute your ex partner's demands, do so under the auspices of trained professionals. Work with assessors or other mental health professionals such as parenting coaches or parenting coordinators whose objectives are always to minimize the impact of parental conflict upon the children while facilitating structures to meet their needs best. Settling differences in court must truly be the very last alternative. Know that you can win the battle yet lose the war. Spending more time with your children does not automatically result in a better relationship.

BARBARA AND BRIAN TALK

Barbara and Brian need to ask themselves: How much is Brian's lack of attention to Barbara's kids under his control? What can he do about this? How much is the access time with his own children subject to discussion and negotiation? What is their sphere of influence? How do Barbara and Brian manage their own preferences in view of the well-being of all the children? How do Barbara's needs and wants figure into conflict between her and Brian's former partner?

In the best-case scenario, Brian would open up a dialogue with his former partner and Barbara would join in the conversation. After understanding the concerns of each person, it would be easier to arrive at mutually acceptable solutions. But what if the best-case scenario is unachievable? What if Brian's former partner is unapproachable?

Seeking to limit the extent of conflict between himself and his former partner, Brian might choose to live under the current access regime. In view of the entire situation, the therapist might help Barbara come to understand that this is a reasonable decision in an unreasonable situation.

This would leave Brian's worry that his children feel they get less attention than his stepchildren, though. In therapy, Brian could learn to broach the subject with his stepchildren as well as his biological children. Perhaps he could learn to conduct a family conference, a meeting, as coached by the therapist. This is what actually happened.

Brian, Barbara and all four children sat around a table in the kitchen of their home. Brian raised his concerns to facilitate hearing the children's perspectives.

Barbara's children were surprised that Brian was in this conundrum. They had thought perhaps he just didn't like them much. They could, now that the situation was out in the open, understand Brian's dilemma and feel bad for him. With a better understanding resulting in a change of expectations, Barbara's children were less affected by Brian's lack of attention.

In this new communication mode, Brian's children admitted feeling jealous about Brian's time spent with Barbara's children. Barbara's children suggested that whenever Brian's children visited for the weekend, Brian and his children could spend time together while they, Barbara's children, spent time with their mother. The children then resolved that on Saturday nights, all six of them would have fun as a family. What had seemed like an insurmountable issue for the parents was easily resolved to the satisfaction of the children.

As for holidays, Barbara was more adamant that they have time together as a whole family and that their time together take place on the designated day. This issue required greater time for her and Brian to discuss her feelings with the therapist. With time and therapy, Barbara was able to realize the importance of resisting conflict in lieu of peace and developing new family traditions. Within two years, their family came to expect and enjoy one of their holidays a day late.

Barbara also learned to stop worrying about Brian's former partner's negative attitude and concentrate more fully on her time with all their children and being a family within their own circle. These matters took several years to work out. Resolving these conflicts began with some very good conversations, flexibility and being able to change perspectives. Brian and Barbara succeeded as a couple. Brian grew close to Barbara's children and took as much pride in their accomplishments as in his own children's achievements.

The Winner's Motto:
I will talk with our children
and spare them adult conflict.

Not Listening

The Sinner's Motto:
What I have to say is more important
than what you have to say.

Some individuals communicate by word, some by deed, some by omission. The issue isn't just *if* we communicate, but *how* we communicate and the *quality* of that communication. We not only have to get a message across, but also it must be accomplished in a way that the receiver can concentrate on the content and not the delivery and make sense of it. We can't be so busy rehearsing our own comebacks that we never really listen to what is being said.

HEARING LOSS

The first issue is hearing. We hear through our ears and our ears are subdivided into three parts: outer, middle and inner. Sound is collected by the outer ear, transferred through the air in the middle ear to the fluid-filled inner ear and transformed into electrical impulses that are interpreted by the brain. Damage to any part of this hearing apparatus can result in hearing loss.

While most people can relate to temporary hearing loss as a result of exposure to explosive sounds or direct physical injury, such as a blow to the head, hearing loss can also be so gradual so as not to be detected. This slow, progressive and often unnoticed hearing loss is referred to as insidious onset. The affected person usually does not perceive him or herself to be suffering from a hearing loss. Though it is gradual, it still affects the person who is missing auditory information.

Insidious onset hearing loss is associated with damage to the inner ear. Drug-induced hearing loss can occur from common medications whose known side effects include the possibility of hearing loss. Noise trauma hearing loss is the outcome of long-term exposure to sounds at high volume, such as loud music at concerts, personal listening devices played at high volume levels or noisy workplaces. The mechanism of inner ear hearing loss is generally associated with damage to the microscopic hairs that line the inner ear. These are responsible for transforming the sound waves within the fluid of the inner ear into electrical impulses which are then interpreted by the brain. Apart from damage to the inner ear from drugs or long-term noise exposure, there also can be insidious onset hearing loss associated with aging.

Insidious onset hearing losses most notably affect hearing of higher pitched sounds first. First to "disappear" are hissing sounds, like "s." In the absence of these higher frequency sound waves, words sound muddy, almost like listening to someone trying to speak under water. Women's voices are normally higher pitched than men's voices, so trying to make sense of a woman's voice in the absence of hearing the high frequency sounds is more difficult and, in the midst of other competing noises, the issue of hearing loss can be overlooked.

This is important when partners express themselves to each other. The most fundamental aspect of communication is hearing. Therapists frequently receive the complaint, "My partner doesn't listen to me," but many do not consider the apparatus of hearing as the likely culprit. Partners and therapists alike are more apt to consider a person not listening as a matter of attitude over ability. When this happens, one spouse feels blamed for the purported bad attitude and feels mislabeled, if not abused. Unfortunately, this compounds the problem for couples in therapy as therapeutic efforts don't produce the desired results and make attending therapy a punishing experience. It is hoped that you and the next couples we focus on choose therapists attuned to matters of hearing loss.

Matthew and Maya's Story

Matthew and Maya were in their mid-thirties and had been together about five years. While Matthew had always been self-absorbed as a person, Maya was becoming increasingly frustrated with him, feeling he was not listening to her. Even during meal times, sitting in each other's company, Maya found herself having to nudge Matthew for responses when she was trying to have a conversation with him.

He always said he was thinking about something else while gazing out to the backyard and hadn't been listening or concentrating on what she was saying. Maya felt disrespected and became angry with Matthew, who in turn felt put down, because he didn't view himself as disrespectful. This circular discussion formed their conflict and mutual resentment built, undermining their intimacy. They sought counseling.

Ethan and Emma's Story

Ethan and Emma, both in their mid-sixties, had been married for many years. Over the years, Ethan had been listening to the television louder and louder. Emma was frustrated having to yell at Ethan to get his attention. She had formed the opinion that he was willfully not listening and she used the loud volume of the TV to support her claim.

Ethan complained that Emma whispered on purpose just so she could complain about his not hearing her. Emma and Ethan's children were upset about the conflict between their parents and convinced them to go to therapy.

Fortunately in both Matthew and Maya's and Ethan and Emma's cases, the therapist wondered about possible hearing loss and asked about related issues.

Matthew was a passionate music lover. In his teens and early twenties, he was an avid concert goer. Loud rock and roll was his favorite musical genre. A few years ago he got his first portable MP3 player and came to love the ability to listen to music anywhere, anytime. He was a junior executive where, in the past, radio music used to be piped in, but now everyone seemed tuned in to their own devices. Matthew told the therapist that he had some ringing in his ears from time to time, particularly after using his portable MP3 player for extended periods at loud levels, but he had never thought it was important.

Ethan was a recently retired accountant. In his office there had been no loud environment, no loud music. He had some health problems and was on a few medications. He recalled that his mother complained about his father's not listening as they grew older, but he didn't feel he was willfully tuning out Emma similar to the way his mother had criticized his father. Emma had her own health problems. She was a former smoker who suffered from emphysema. Her lung capacity was not the same as when she was younger and her voice had grown more aspirated and breathy with age.

The therapist explored the spouses' personal histories as couples and as individuals going back to their childhoods. To the therapist, nothing appeared of significance to explain their marital problems.

However, in both cases the therapist suspected hearing loss to be at the root of the relationship difficulties.

It was disconcerting to the therapist that Matthew seemed to have difficulty hearing Maya during their session when the two of them were seated on the same couch facing the therapist. Matthew's ability to converse with Maya improved when the therapist had him sit on the opposite couch, facing her. From that vantage point, Matthew was able to rely on visual cues, seeing when Maya was about to talk and when she was actually talking. With those visual cues, Matthew leaned in toward her to listen more attentively, but this took some effort.

In Ethan and Emma's case, the therapist theorized that their communication issues were compounded by Emma's higher, airy-sounding voice. The side effects of Emma's emphysema compounded with Ethan's hearing loss. The therapist advised that when Emma wanted Ethan's attention, she would have to turn down the television volume to reduce its competition with her voice. She would also have to try to speak with a lower tone to her voice.

Both Ethan and Matthew were advised to see their doctors for referrals to audiologists. Now alerted to their problems, both were amazed at their degree of hearing loss. Matthew also had to come to terms with the fact that his hearing loss was likely self-induced, the result of years of listening to music at loud volumes. He was advised by the audiologist to protect his residual hearing by not using his portable MP3 player and trying to keep the volume low in other situations.

*The therapist explained the importance to Maya and Emma
of having their partners' attention first before trying to say
something, of reducing competing sounds before conversing and
sitting or standing facing each other so their partners could rely
on visual cues as well as auditory information.*

In both cases, the issue was not attitude but hearing ability
and in view of hearing loss, both couples needed to make structural
changes to facilitate their communication. Working with the therapist, the animosity and resentment within these couples went away.

PERSONALITY VARIABLES CREATING CONFLICT

As we've discussed, issues of communication come up repeatedly.
It should be noted, though, that when some couples raise the issue
of communication, they are actually communicating well. They just
don't like what they hear or they can't believe what they are hearing,
thinking the other partner misunderstood what was said or the other
partner misspoke.

While many people believe their problems relate to issues of communication, this isn't necessarily the case. You and your partner may
be communicating very well but have different attitudes, beliefs or
expectations. You can communicate all you want in these situations,
but if your partner is inflexible, sitting in front of each other extolling
the virtues of your opinions, needs or wants is useless. In these situations, you likely require some degree of counseling or therapy to
uncover where your respective views come from or why one partner
is so self-centered or angry. Therapy is aimed at helping spouses to
learn about their attitudes, problem-solving styles, unmet needs/
wants and ways of viewing the world that get in the way of working
together toward mutual goals and a fulfilling marriage.

For instance, if one parent is permissive by nature and the other authoritarian, they have such radically different styles that neither can appreciate the other's view. In these situations, partners need to learn that their different styles—not their ability to communicate—are the issue in their conflicts. They need to learn how to align their respective styles to parent more effectively together.

In another example, if a person grew up in a family where he or she was indulged, had few expectations and could get away with any sort of behavior, then that partner may have formed an opinion that his or her needs and wants come before other people's needs and wants. This opinion might be that person's view of life as determined by his or her formative experiences as a child. Take that point of view into a relationship with someone who expects to have his or her needs and wants addressed alongside the other partner's, as opposed to second to the other partner's, and the relationship is ripe for conflict. Learning to communicate will be of little value under these circumstances. Rather, such individuals will have to learn how their formative experiences shaped their views of themselves and their places in the world.

Help with communication doesn't make a self-centered person less self-centered or a person prone to drama less histrionic. These issues are beyond matters of hearing or communication and constitute the core of one's being, likely an outcome of how a person was raised and what the person was exposed to while growing up. Couples therapy is beneficial in these situations, but it requires a deeper and more exploratory type of therapy than sitting and listening to "he said, she said," with each clarifying and re-clarifying what he or she meant or wanted from the other.

These matters are driven by more deep-seated personality variables and are often more challenging to correct. To remedy these problems, the partners must be able to self-reflect and, if unable, must trust the information provided by the therapist with respect to their points of view or ways of interpreting the world that interfere with their intimate relationships. Depending on the severity and sometimes the kind of personality issue a person possesses, success can be hard fought, minimal and, at times, elusive or nonexistent.

Therapy can be helpful to many people, but not everyone will benefit from it. In these circumstances, therapy can prove psychologically and emotionally freeing for individuals who learn that their partners have personality dispositions not consistent with the view of others and which create conflict as a result.

EFFECTIVE COMMUNICATION

Be aware that altering one's personality or view of the world is usually a more difficult task than learning to communicate. Personalities tend to be quite stable over time and resistant to change. Although personalities are difficult to alter, behavior can more easily be subject to change. Just because you see the world a particular way doesn't mean that you can't learn to live or behave in the world and with others in a different way. You or your partner's personality and disposition must be amenable to self-reflection, taking responsibility—at times even for things you may not fully understand or appreciate—and learning to adopt new behaviors to get along better with others.

Improving one's communication skills or learning to manage one's personality variables that lead to conflict is a process that takes considerable time, requires practice and may feel unnatural. In the beginning, less is more, until practice develops your strength and ability. Learning new skills is not a function of belief, attitude or expectation. It is only a function of practice—learning and using new skills and developing those skills slowly over time.

Learning to address one's personality variables and using communication skills to resolve conflict relies on practice. If any attitude is required, it is in terms of a willingness to learn and develop these new skills. In the scheme of things there are six key communication skills to learn as a couple:

1. Limit distractions
2. Sweat the delivery

3. Prepare to listen

4. Show that you got it

5. Respond to dig deeper

6. Take responsibility

Let's look more closely at these items:

1. Limit distractions

Often when we seek to communicate, we are distracted by our own thoughts, other activities, noise and children. It is difficult if not impossible at times, to concentrate enough to take in that which is transmitted. When you want to communicate something that you feel, you need to make sure you have your partner's attention. This is best achieved if the two of you are alone, away from interruptions and in a setting that allows you to see each other directly. Depending on the seriousness or importance of the issue to be discussed, it might actually be better to set an appointment with each other, a specified length of time set aside specifically to address the matter. In terms of limiting distractions, consider hunger, fatigue and bodily functions. As minor as some of these factors leading to distraction might seem, they can impede effective communication and should be prevented or handled in advance of your meeting.

2. Sweat the delivery

You need your partner to concentrate on what you have to say, not how you say it. To this end, you have to manage the intensity of your feelings. If you are angry with your partner, yelling, shouting, barraging or blaming will not help your partner receive your message. If you are upset or sad, crying might overwhelm your partner with the intensity of your emotions, impeding his or her ability to concentrate on your message. Similarly, if you are so nervous that you are giggling or laughing, you may provide the impression that your issues are not as significant as they might truly be. It is important to get a grip on your feelings and find a way to manage them so that they don't inadvertently intrude and become the focal point of your discussion instead of your real issue.

If your delivery concentrates exclusively on the real or perceived misdeed of your partner and you are seeking to admonish, confront or hold your partner solely accountable, then you are likely to meet with resistance. It is helpful to talk about what has happened, how you interpreted what went on and how you were affected by it. Take a similar approach to whatever your issue may be. Address the issue and how you are perturbed by it. Do not assume that your partner necessarily behaves in certain ways to annoy, upset or aggravate you. Your partner may not understand the impact of his or her behavior upon you and so you should take an informational approach to advise your partner of the issues that have affected you from your perspective.

Comment on your own role in the issue. Maybe you haven't made yourself clear in the past and have created confusion in the mind of your partner; maybe you have expected your partner to anticipate your feelings and wants; maybe the management of your own emotions has not been appropriate and you need to take responsibility. Very often you both are involved in co-creating miscommunication and an interpersonal problem. Address your part in it.

If you are concerned that either your feelings or your partner's feelings will get in the way of a smooth delivery, meta-communicate. Tell your partner that what you have to say is difficult and that you will do your best to control your emotions. You may have to tell your partner you are concerned about how he or she will react to what you have to say and that you would appreciate the opportunity to speak freely and fully to express your concerns and that you hope your partner can listen to your entire story, as difficult as some portions may be to hear.

You may have to negotiate with your partner about how your partner will handle him or herself if he or she becomes upset. This can include taking breaks, conceding to disagree and allowing your partner to take some time—from a few minutes to several days—to think over what you said before responding. Some people can process their emotions very quickly and accurately while others require more time to collect their thoughts and process emotions. Neither way is inherently good or bad, just different, and your partner must feel that it is acceptable to take whatever time he or she feels is necessary. Taking time must not automatically be seen as being passive, non-reactive or avoiding.

3. Prepare to listen

Perhaps you have rehearsed what you want to say, anticipating a heated conversation. You want to get your own point across to "win" the discussion, a discussion likely entered into as a debate or with the threat of being on the defensive, feeling you have to protect yourself from blame, rightly or wrongly. You feel a need either to commence your attack or have a defense at the ready. Either way, you are not prepared to listen, really listen, to the other person, because you are either preparing yourself for battle or rehearsing your part. It is a challenge in this circumstance to be fully present and hear what the other person is saying. However, if you do not hear what the other person is saying, one of three things might happen:

    a. The person who feels he or she is not being heard will escalate the intensity in an effort to break through.

b. The person who feels he or she is not being heard might withdraw, believing continuing to be useless.

c. You may misinterpret what has been said and thus your reply might not be appropriate.

In any of these situations the outcome will be poor and the issue will remain unresolved.

To communicate effectively, you must suspend your interest in what you have to say in favor of receiving and being fully present for what the other person has to say. You do not have to agree with or like what is being said, but you can't be so busy thinking about what you want to say that you don't hear what is being said to you. If you are concerned about forgetting what you want to say, write it down. Make notes in advance of your meeting so you can be sure to remember your concerns and you can thoroughly concentrate on listening to the concerns of your partner.

4. Show that you understand

Once your partner has said what he or she needs to say and without interruption, you need to demonstrate that you have received his or her message and have understood it correctly. Check this by putting what your partner has said into your own words and asking if this is what he or she intended. Doing this puts your partner at ease that his or her intended message has been received. Again, you don't have to accept any part, but you need to indicate you have correctly received the intended message and meaning.

5. Respond to dig deeper

Don't settle on just what your partner has said; go further to understand at a more meaningful level, even if you don't agree. Before providing your argument or your own issue, dig deeper. Take a "what if" point of view. What if your partner was correct, either about you or about the situation? Explore your partner's perspective. Ask for other instances or examples. Ask your partner what you could have done differently to mitigate the issue. Ask your partner how things would have been different if you had followed your partner's advice. Take the opportunity to learn more from your partner's perspective. In so doing, you might come to learn that even if you assess your contribution to distress to be minimal, a small change on your part can be highly conducive to a different, more amenable outcome.

You might believe your transgression to be small, but that doesn't mean it is inconsequential to your partner. Something seemingly small may still have a significant consequence. Take this to heart and learn from your partner what will be more helpful in the future. Explore your contribution to distress from your partner's perspective and consider your partner's feedback in terms of how to make your relationship better.

6. Take responsibility

Apologizing for your contribution to distress as explained by your partner and for your impact upon your partner is not the same as letting your partner off the hook for his or her contribution and impact. Can you really expect your partner to take responsibility for his or her contribution to distress if you don't take responsibility for yours?

If you have caused upset or pain, acknowledge your part in it. If you have trouble understanding your part, then say so, but indicate you are still sorry for any part you played. Demonstrate that you can act or respond differently to that kind of situation, if encountered again in the future. If you are unsure that you will be able to recognize your contribution in the future and though it is preferable that you take full responsibility for managing yourself, you and your partner can come to an agreement that your partner will point out the issue to you in the moment to bring it to your attention so you can deal with it more effectively. You agree to accept the reminder and direction for improved behavior.

Taking responsibility for one's contribution to distress and being amenable to act differently in the future breeds satisfaction and causes one's partner to feel that he or she is being taken seriously. This is validating. It creates hope and improves relationships.

Once this conversation is accomplished, with your partner's consent it is time to start the process again, beginning with another concern or matter to be addressed or resolved. Start by limiting distractions. Either of you might be fatigued by this point and might need a break to use the bathroom or take time to process what just transpired. It might be that the matters between you have been resolved. Perhaps, by suspending a defensive reaction, you learned something about yourself that, if changed, would create the conditions for a more mutually satisfying relationship. Maybe the issue you wanted to raise is now redundant. You might already have rescued your relationship by listening and tweaking your own behavior. Realizing that your co-creation of the problem requires you to take responsibility for your contribution to distress may be all that is necessary to turn your marriage into a success.

Nancy and Roy's Story

Nancy and Roy lived in a nice house, puttered in their garden and had three grown sons who had children of their own. The grandchildren occasionally visited and could be seen helping in the garden.

Nancy and Roy made marriage look easy and their younger neighbors admired their relationship. Although they made it look easy, Nancy and Roy knew differently.

Relating wasn't always as simple as it looked. There was a time when Nancy and Roy didn't think they would make it as a couple, let alone raise three boys together and enjoy many grandchildren. If someone had asked them at the beginning of their marriage if they thought they would enjoy a happy, fulfilling relationship, both would have guessed not. They had serious issues that had put their now good marriage at risk.

Early in their relationship Nancy became pregnant. They were just in their teens at the time. The child was given up for adoption. This child was never spoken of; the baby was their secret, not even known to their other three sons.

After a tumultuous early start, Roy and Nancy found each other again. Roy was rough around the edges then and Nancy still wasn't sure about herself. But they found their way back to each other and eventually married. They started fresh, but with skeletons in their closet.

Getting pregnant again opened old wounds for Nancy. She felt she couldn't put up with Roy's cantankerous ways and began to mourn the loss of her firstborn son, given up for adoption. With the birth of her second son (first to everyone else) she became depressed. Nancy internalized her anger with Roy, believing that if not for him, she would not have gotten pregnant the first time and wouldn't be missing her firstborn, wondering about him, these thoughts rekindled by the birth of this new boy.

She and Roy stopped having sex and she insisted he change. At that point in their lives, he would have to become the kind of man who would be acceptable to her. Roy had no idea how to be the kind of man his wife would accept. They struggled for years while raising their "first" boy. From angry and loud to silent and distant, they argued. There was even a period of heavy drinking and nights when Roy didn't make it home. Those were very troubled times.

Crashing his car was the turning point. Roy joined Alcoholics Anonymous as a result, a program he continued to attend. His attendance now was not to maintain his sobriety, though, but to be there for others, the way others had been there for him. He was the senior statesman in the group, a source of accomplishment who provided a sense of duty. His sons knew he went to rehabilitation, but never the whole story. The eldest was too young to remember when his dad stopped drinking. The two other brothers were born after Roy got his act together.

It was after committing to AA that Roy began seeing things differently. Slowly he began taking responsibility for himself and he acknowledged his role in the hidden first pregnancy he shared with Nancy. Although it hung in the air between them, it had never been discussed after the birth and adoption. The secret precipitated Nancy's depression; Roy's attending AA brought it out, giving Roy the courage to confront his past and acknowledge the pain of a secret with his wife. Together they mourned the loss of the son they would never know.

It took five years for Nancy to come to terms with her life and decisions. Roy's opening up was the permission Nancy needed to open up too. She expressed her anger at Roy and the more her anger came out in the open, the more her depression lifted. With his AA group to support him, Roy was able to withstand the intensity of her feelings. It was only after her intensity began to wane and her depression lifted that Nancy was able to acknowledge her role in the pregnancy. She admitted that as much as she blamed Roy for it, she knew she was looking to be loved and gave herself to him thinking it would win her a place in his heart at the time and provide what had been missing in her life. Only after all that did they find a permanent place in each other's heart.

The rest of their life together did not just fall into place. Roy and Nancy struggled with many things along the way. They had a scare with their third son who was seriously ill for a long period and then there was the time Roy's factory shut down and they feared losing their home.

After learning how to communicate, they addressed their fears directly and they learned to talk to each other first when upset, worried and even joyous. Although they missed their secret firstborn, Roy and Nancy believed that he had grown up to be a fine man in his adoptive family. They were proud of their other three boys' accomplishments and were happy with the quality of their relationship.

It took time for this couple to rebalance their ledgers—those things about which they felt good versus those things about which they did not. Having overcome much adversity, they felt satisfied to share with each other their lives and love.

The Winner's Motto:
I'm listening. Please talk.

Moving Forward

When you chose this book you were probably looking to find a solution to serious problems in your relationship with your partner, but if you have read the book through to this conclusion, you must now realize that as much as you needed to learn about your partner, you have had to learn some important things about yourself. These are your own sins, the ones you need to claim.

Do you blame others for problems originating with yourself? Are you still so attached to your parents they overwhelm you, making you still feel like a child, managing your life and that of your partner? Are you so self-absorbed that you can't clean up after yourself? Do you put your friends ahead of your partner? Perhaps you like to control the money or believe you don't have to be accountable for your own spending. Maybe you are seeing someone else or are preoccupied with something else. Have you been deluded by alcohol or drugs, thinking them not a problem, making excuse after excuse, secretly knowing you are addicted? Do you think might is right and winning is paramount, regardless of the consequences or who gets hurt? Maybe you have lost your voice or never had one and you inadvertently give the impression that nothing matters, because you never speak up for yourself. Have you been thinking that if not for the children, all would be well or that your children are the only ones who matter? Even if you talk to your partner, do you listen? What's your sin?

You can have multiple sins. Many sins naturally go together: Trouble setting boundaries with parents as well as friends; not cleaning up after yourself and thinking you don't have to share; abuse of drugs or alcohol often brings violence and depression; blaming the children might tie in with not listening. Do you have multiple sins?

Looking back at some of the couples we've discussed, these issues can be divided into three types: communication problems, personality problems and a combination of both.

Darrel (sin 1) had a view of women and relationships that was skewed by having grown up with an abusive father. While he needed to learn to communicate more courteously, he also had to come to understand how his personality was negatively affecting his relationship with Sara. Fortunately Darrel was receptive to couples therapy and made substantial changes to his behavior. He learned that rather than projecting blame on his wife, he had to take responsibility for his contribution to distress.

Margaret's mother (sin 2) was dependent upon Margaret as well as being self-absorbed. Therefore, Margaret's mother had personality problems that affected Margaret's relationship with her husband, Martin. Margaret needed to understand her mother's problems and assert boundaries. She and Martin had to learn to communicate more effectively with each other.

Tony and Maria (sin 2) needed to learn to talk with each other and then to set boundaries. Tony needed to learn what to say to his parents, his mother in particular, in order to assert their independence as a couple. There were no evil players here, just the need to identify one's issues and communicate them effectively, non-offensively and non-defensively. Tony was able to do a great job with the help of a script with which to practice.

Frank and Molly (sin 3) were doomed from the start. Both had serious personality issues. Dependent Molly would never get her needs met by self-absorbed Frank. Talk was useless. Needy Molly needed more than Frank would ever provide.

Michael (sin 4) felt he could use his charms to put demands on Jolene, who eventually got fed up. Meanwhile Sandhu and Sarit as well as Dominique and Marta needed to learn to talk with each other and clarify their pasts and expectations. As they did, their issues dissolved.

Charlie and Millie (sin 5) demonstrated how sometimes a combination of personality and communication issues creates relationship problems. Millie acted with a sense of entitlement and she had to learn to listen to Charlie's distress about financial issues. Millie had to realize how her belief that she could have what she wanted created health problems for Charlie and together they needed to learn to talk this out and find more acceptable strategies for managing their money.

Katie (sin 6) demonstrated issues with both communication and personality variables. She had unmet needs stemming from early childhood, undermining her sense of self-worth. She was unable to make her needs known to her husband, Todd, who also contributed to the distress and distancing felt in their marriage. This amplified issues for Katie. It was only when she set the stage to talk with her husband that things changed.

Keith (sin 7) wasn't just alcoholic but also very self-absorbed. His alcohol use only served to fuel his pursuit of self serving behavior to the point of sabotaging his marriage. Alcohol or drug use and personality issues can interact with negative results.

Derek (sin 8) pushed the limits while growing up and broke through the limits by physically and sexually assaulting his wife, Joanne. His personality variables were some of the most severe of any individual we've examined. His issues were beyond being fixed on the basis of facilitating communication. The severity of his personality defects was such that he would never accept looking at himself as the problem.

Stu and Elaine (sin 8) would really benefit from assistance with communication. They needed to learn to use more appropriate words more effectively. They needed to learn the six steps of effective communication. These strategies might slow down discussion, but they would facilitate improved understanding so that the partners could more reasonably resolve differences. In so doing, they also presented themselves as more appropriate role models to their children. For Stu and Elaine, it eased their son's concerns for their well-being.

Dan and Carey (sin 9) were otherwise reasonable people whose lives were set off course by an unplanned pregnancy. They had to come to terms with this and learn to discuss their feelings frankly with each other in order to overcome their opinions about the pregnancy and their lives together.

Larry and Leticia (sin 9) were impacted by a combination of personality and communication problems. Larry was authoritarian in his parenting style and Leticia was permissive. Their childhood pasts influenced their view of how children should behave and how parents should parent. They had to learn about their respective viewpoints, how to talk about these matters and how to parent more effectively than either was doing. This took considerable self-reflection and lessons in effective communication.

Matthew and Maya and Ethan and Emma (sin 10) are examples of couples who experienced affected communication due to hearing loss. The issue wasn't the delivery but the reception, by virtue of structural hearing problems. No amount of counseling from a perspective of attitudinal issues will address a problem that is medical or health related. Fortunately, the counselor from whom these two couples sought advice had an appreciation of health-related issues and determined that health problems were interfering with the relationships.

Nancy and Roy (sin 10) faced many hardships in their marriage and had to overcome many issues. With time and work devoted to the relationship, Nancy and Roy made changes and overcame their problems. They experienced a rich, deep satisfaction in their marriage.

To rescue your marriage, you must come to terms with your own contribution to marital distress and seek to change it. Admitting and taking responsibility for your sins does not mean your partner has no sins, but by starting the process you don't have to wait, wondering who will go first. Of the things you can feel good about, you can feel good about taking responsibility and seeking to turn your marriage around.

Maybe you are frightened that if you take the first step your partner will not reciprocate, may leave you or disclose your sins to others. Maybe you are frightened your partner will point a finger at you to say, "I told you so and now you admit it—you're the bad one." These are all reasons not to go first, not to try. But do you really want to do the same things over and over again, knowing that doing them likely won't improve your marriage?

Taking responsibility takes risks. You may have more turmoil and upheaval in your life. Your standard of living may go down. You may fight over the care of the children. It is possible that, as you might fear, you will be subject to an escalation of abuse and violence. If so, you must protect yourself and your children by finding a safe haven.

I do not advocate harm. I do not advocate taking foolhardy risks.

I do advocate careful consideration of your situation, planning and forethought before action. I advocate safety first.

If you are in a dilemma, wanting to take responsibility for your contribution to distress but concerned for the consequences, then seek professional help. Get help from people who specialize in your area of concern. You have the right to ask any prospective counselor about his or her training, experience and expertise. You also have the right to ask about costs, availability, typical duration of service, typical outcomes, location and service delivery policies (the rules by which they deliver service).

Ask the professional to help you develop a realistic view of your situation and your role within it. Realize that you have to come to terms with your situation and your role. Get help planning how to address not only your situation but also the different circumstances that may arise.

If you are in an abusive relationship, seek counseling from a professional with specific expertise in domestic violence and power imbalances. If your matter is financial, seek counseling from someone with knowledge in finances and financial planning. If your matter is drug or alcohol related, seek help from professionals with expertise in addiction. Narcotics Anonymous and Alcoholics Anonymous are excellent sources of help for many. If you are the loved one of an alcoholic, seek support from Alateen or Al-Anon. Take your issues seriously enough to address them and deal with them. Even if your partner accuses you, you will have the benefit of knowing you have improved yourself relative to those issues. You won't have to hide from yourself when it comes time to tally up your ledger.

There are no guarantees as to how your partner will handle your change. You are seeking to rescue your marriage, but there are no guarantees what the final outcome will be. Life contains uncertainties. As much as we like our structures and routines, as much as we like to know what to expect, life is anything but predictable. Things change. Illness comes, people die, the economy declines and rebounds, bad weather comes and goes. We can try to hold steadfast against change, but if it doesn't work, we need to have a plan and be prepared. Your relationship will likely change someday. It may not be for the better or it may not be under your influence. It may be by accident or it may be by design. Where will you be?

Relationship rescue is about taking personal responsibility. If you aren't equipped to handle an adult relationship based on the incidental learning that comes from growing up in a family structure, then you may have some learning to do in order to improve yourself in your marital relationship. This is neither good nor bad. It just is.

When you don't have the skills, take on the task of learning what to do to make things work. Get egos out of the way, take turns, practice and support each other through mistakes.

My wish for you and your partner who feel in need of a marriage rescue is that you learn to tackle the problems and issues which have gotten in the way of your sharing a fulfilling relationship; admit where you have work to do; find the experts to address the work; take it on; make the needed changes.

Take responsibility for your own sins first, then work toward having the kind of relationship you dream of having.

THE TEN DEADLY SINS:
Sinners' And Winners' Mottos

SIN	SINNER'S MOTTO	WINNER'S MOTTO
Blaming	It's not me; it's you.	I take responsibility for my behavior and avoid blaming my partner.
Letting the In-Laws Interfere	Why can't my mom hang around?	It's up to me to set boundaries with my parents.
Putting Your Friends Ahead of Your Partner	What's wrong with my friends?	I put my partner before my friends and find balance in meeting my needs.
Not Sharing the Chores	Clean it yourself.	I clean what I help make dirty and appreciate that chores are meant to be shared.

SIN	SINNER'S MOTTO	WINNER'S MOTTO
Thinking It's Your Money	If I earned it, I can spend it.	Our relationship is richer when we share and plan together.
Stepping Out on Your Partner	We are only friends; we never had sex.	I am reserved for my partner only.
Abusing Alcohol or Drugs	I can quit anytime I want.	I am fully present in my relationship with body, mind and spirit.
Using Violence in Any Form	I win.	We respect each other as our mutual priority.
Making Your Children the Problem	Children are a pain.	I will talk with our children and spare them adult conflict.
Not Listening	What I have to say is more important than what you have to say.	I'm listening. Please talk.

RESOURCES

Always ask about your potential service provider's credentials, years of practice, expertise, experience, fees, hours of operation, availability, affiliations and policy on confidentiality.

ALCOHOL/DRUG ADDICTION SUPPORT

- Al-Anon
  http://www.al-anon.org/
- Alateen
  http://www.al-anon.alateen.org/for-alateen
- Alcoholics Anonymous
  http://www.aa.org
- Narcotics Anonymous
  http://www.na.org/

FAMILY COUNSELING SERVICES

- Association of Jewish Family & Children's Agencies (AJFCA)
  http://www.ajfca.org/
- Family Service Canada
  http://www.familyservicecanada.org/
- Islamic Social Services Association
  http://www.issausa.org/

FINANCIAL COUNSELING

- Academy of Financial Divorce Specialists
  http://www.afds.ca
- Institute for Divorce Financial Analysts
  https://www.institutedfa.com/

LEGAL ADVICE

- International Academy of Collaborative Professionals
  http://www.collaborativepractice.com/

MARRIAGE AND FAMILY THERAPISTS

- American Association for Marriage and Family Therapy
  http://www.aamft.org
- Gary Direnfeld
  www.yoursocialworker.com
- Registry of Marriage and Family Therapists in Canada, Inc.
  http://www.marriageandfamily.ca

WOMEN'S SHELTERS AND SUPPORT SERVICES

- National Domestic Violence Hotline (United States)
  http://www.thehotline.org/
- YWCA (Canada)
  http://ywcacanada.ca
- YWCA (United States)
  http://www.ywca.org